Contents

Preface

This much revised and extended fourth edition examines the development of supply-side economics, assesses the performance of recent supply-side policies and considers the future of supply-side policies. It contains detailed information and clear analysis on an area which, to date, has often been dealt with all too briefly in many economics textbooks. Given the increased importance attached by governments to supply-side policies and by the new A level and AS level specifications, this is a welcome new edition written by two experts in the field.

It should prove to be particularly useful for students studying for AQA's Modules 2, 5 and 6, Edexcel's Units 3 and 6, OCR's Modules 2883 and 2887, HND and degree courses.

Susan Grant
Series Editor

Introduction

'Supply-side theory showed that macroeconomics works just like microeconomics – through changes in relative prices, not by changes in demand. It may take economists a while longer to absorb this idea. When they do, the supply-side revolution will be complete.'
Business Week, 1999

The term 'supply-side economics' was first coined in 1976 to describe economic policies designed to influence output and employment through their impact on the supply-side, as opposed to the demand-side, of the economy. *Supply-side policies cause a shift to the right of the aggregate supply curve leading to greater output at lower prices*, so long as the economy is below the full employment level.

Although the term 'supply-side economics' is relatively new the basic concept is not. Ever since 1945, governments of both political persuasions have attempted to strengthen the supply-side in their quest for more rapid economic growth. *Until 1979, however, supply-side policy took second place to demand management policy.* While successive governments recognised the potential benefits of directly promoting the supply-side of the economy, it was generally believed that the major contribution governments could make to economic prosperity was to keep – through the active use of *demand-management policy* – the economy as close as possible to 'full-employment'. By ensuring that aggregate demand was always high enough to allow firms to work at full capacity, it was argued, governments could create a stable, supportive economic environment in which firms had the confidence and incentive to invest for growth.

In the period 1945–79, supply-side policy thus played an essentially supporting role, with governments intervening directly in the supply-side in areas where a high and stable level of aggregate demand did not, of itself, appear to be sufficient to stimulate investment and growth.

Underpinning both demand-management and supply-side policies during the so-called 'Keynesian era' was a deep-seated distrust of the free market and a feeling that the 'invisible hand' was unable to co-ordinate economic activity and achieve growth. Without the active involvement of paternalistic government, it was concluded, it would be impossible to achieve economic success.

1

Thus demand-management policy was considered so important because it was felt that, in the absence of compensating adjustments in monetary and fiscal policy, the level of aggregate demand would tend to fluctuate wildly, rarely reaching the level necessary for full-employment. Similarly, supply-side policy took the form of intervening in the decision-making of the private sector, on the grounds that such decisions would otherwise be irrational and shortsighted.

This pessimistic view of free markets was successfully challenged by the *new classical economists* in the late 1970s, who provided the intellectual inspiration for the economic policies that have been pursued since 1979. The new classical economists reasserted the power of free markets to deliver economic prosperity, denying that governments could systematically increase output and employment through the use of either demand-management or interventionist supply-side policies. They argued that demand-management policies ultimately resulted in inflation, concluding that such policies were futile and misguided. More radically still, they rejected Keynesian notions of *market failure*, claiming that the best way to strengthen the supply-side was not via direct government intervention but rather by cutting taxes and liberating otherwise vital market forces from cloying state bureaucracy.

Although Keynesians and new classical economists remain sharply divided over the appropriate role of government in the economy, *both schools of thought agree that the subject matter of 'supply-side economics' is the economics of growth.*

The various factors that could be utilised to stimulate growth were traditionally reflected in the political nature of the ruling party. In the UK, Labour was more associated with Keynesian prescriptions for growth and the Conservatives, from 1979, with new classical approaches. All this has changed. The election of the new Labour administration has seen a party willing to embrace both policy perspectives. In particular the last few years has seen a switch in emphasis towards improving the competitiveness of the UK via innovation and developing of the knowledge-based economy.

In the light of the supply-side policies undertaken, this book examines the most important reasons why Britain has fallen behind in the 'growth race' and considers the policies that have been deployed in recent years in an attempt to stem Britain's relative economic decline.

Chapter One examines Britain's supply-side performance, both relative to historical trends and in comparison with our major trading partners.

Chapter Two explores the determinants of economic growth and links this to the supply-side performance of the UK economy, highlighting the role of training and education, capital investment and technological progress.

Chapter Three gives an overview of the supply-side policies undertaken within the British economy between 1945 and 2000 examining the Keynesian, new classical and 'Third Way' approaches.

Chapters Four to Six appraise the performance of recent supply-side policy in a number of areas such as improving market efficiency, tax reform, labour market reform and the development of investment innovation.

Chapter Seven considers one of the more dynamic areas of the UK economy, that of the small firms sector, and the supply-side policies that have been developed to improve this sector's performance.

Chapter 8 widens the scope of supply-side economics to develop the external influences that have impacted on UK supply-side performance.

Finally, we offer some insights into the likely future impact of the supply-side revolution and the areas to which supply-side policies have still to improve the effectiveness of markets.

Chapter One

Britain's supply-side performance

'Other countries have far greater problems than we have.'
Sir Edward Heath

Introduction

Politicians and economists often talk about the 'supply-side' of the economy. Ministers claim that their policies are designed to 'strengthen the supply-side'. Economists refer to improvements or emerging weaknesses in the 'supply-side' performance of the economy. Implicit in such statements is the idea that the 'supply-side' relates to Britain's basic economic competitiveness; that is, the country's ability to produce goods and services that consumers want, at a price they are prepared to pay.

The simplest way to express the same basic notion in more familiar, textbook terms is to think of a simple aggregate supply and demand diagram (see Figure 1). The aggregate supply schedule (AS) shows how much firms in the economy will produce at different price levels (P), while the aggregate demand schedule (AD) shows the quantities of output (Y) that the nation as a whole (ie, households, businesses and government taken together) want to buy at different price levels. The 'supply-side', therefore, is the part of the economy which lies behind the AS schedule; that is, the companies and workers engaged in the production of goods and services.

From year to year, AD fluctuates up and down, often causing quite sharp changes in total output (Y) which are independent of developments on the supply-side. But, in the long run, it is more fundamental changes on the supply-side of the economy (eg, new products and processes, better educated workers, more efficient plant and equipment) that allow economies to enjoy ever-higher levels of output. Bitter experience has taught us that, if pumping up demand through higher government spending and rapid credit creation were the route to lasting economic prosperity, Britain would be one of the richest countries in the developed world. But as Table 1 shows, Britain had steadily fallen from its ranking as the richest country in Europe to below average in the European Union by the mid-1990s.

However, since the mid-1990s the UK's GDP per capita as a percentage of the EU average has improved. Some see this as a result of

4

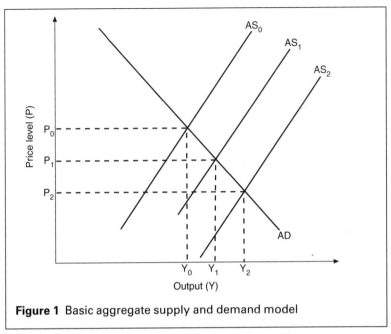

Figure 1 Basic aggregate supply and demand model

the supply-side reforms undertaken over the past twenty years, others however have noted that the decline in the EU average GDP following the re-unification of Germany has pushed the UK higher up the EU GDP per head table as a percentage of the EU average.

Within the context of the AS–AD model, underlying improvements in the supply-side manifest themselves as a continuous, rightward shift in the AS schedule over time (eg, from AS_0 to AS_1 to AS_2), steadily

Table 1 *Per capita* GDP (as % of EU average)

Country	1960	1995	1999
Japan	44.7	186.5	142.8
Denmark	123.2	144.4	142.0
Germany	123.8	127.6	116.3
Luxembourg	158.0	138.8	183.0
United States	268.7	123.8	143.2
France	126.9	115.5	108.2
Belgium	115.4	114.2	109.8
Italy	75.2	88.2	90.8
Netherlands	97.0	108.7	108.2
UK	131.1	87.7	102.9

Source: *European Economy.*

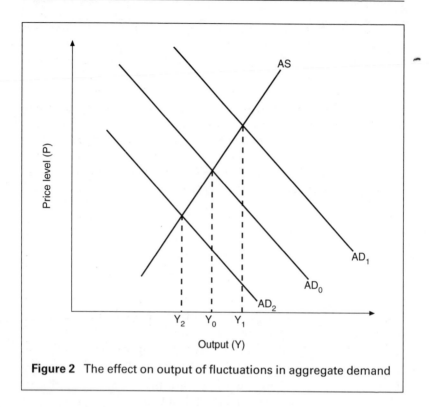

Figure 2 The effect on output of fluctuations in aggregate demand

increasing the quantity of output that firms supply at any given level of AD.

Somewhat confusingly, when professional economists speak of 'economic growth', they often mean nothing more than the change in output over a relatively short period (eg, one year). You may have read newspaper reports along the following lines: 'The Treasury today forecast 2 per cent growth over the next twelve months'; or 'The Opposition leader again declared that, due to the government's mishandling of the economy, Britain will suffer the slowest growth of any major industrial country this year'. However, as Figure 2 suggests, changes in economic growth over such short periods are driven primarily by fluctuations in AD (eg, from AD_0 to AD_1 or to AD_2).

Output and unemployment

Figure 3 illustrates diagrammatically the cyclical pattern that the economy tends to follow. The broken line represents actual output, while the solid line shows the underlying, long-run trend growth in the economy's productive capacity. It is this **'natural rate of output'**, rather than the actual, year-to-year level, which is influenced by changes in the supply-side. During boom years, when the growth of output is accelerating above its natural rate, unemployment steadily falls and actual output is driven above the natural rate of output. Companies have to work nearer to full capacity; bottlenecks appear in the economy; unemployment drops and firms suffer labour shortages, leading them to bid up wage levels; inflation accelerates. Once the boom has peaked and the economy moves into recession, the growth in output slumps below that of the natural rate, possibly even becoming negative, as in 1980–81 and 1990–91. Unemployment mounts, as many firms lay off unneeded workers; others go out of business altogether; inflation slows.

This account of the 'stop-go', 'boom-bust' cycles followed by market economies underscores the key relationship on the supply-side of the economy between output and unemployment. It is interesting to note that the UK appeared to adopt a different approach to 'stop-go' management during the 1990s with economic policy attempting to steer the economy on a much more consistent long-term growth path. Thus slumps appear to be shallower, and booms less marked. Evidence of this can be seen in the downturn in the UK economy during 1997 and the upturn thereafter. In 1997, when the world economy faltered, the UK economy did not go into recession. Similarly when the UK

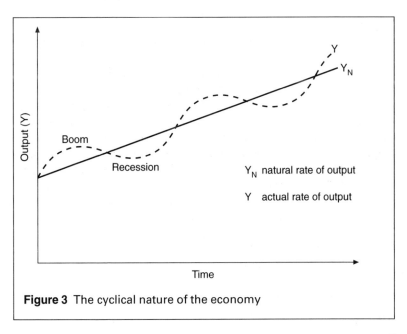

Figure 3 The cyclical nature of the economy

economy showed signs of overheating during 1999/2000, the Bank of England's monetary committee has sought to dampen economic activity before it got out of hand.

By now it should be evident that *rising output, of itself, does not signal an improvement in the supply-side of the economy.* Any country, provided that it first undergoes a deep recession, can temporarily enjoy a period of 'economic growth', simply by allowing an expansion in AD to mop up under-utilised resources and temporarily propel actual output above its natural rate – whether or not that natural rate of output has in fact increased.

In terms of the supply-side of the economy, *what matters is the growth of the natural rate of output; that is, the long-run rate of economic growth that can be sustained over time.* Short-run fluctuations in the growth of actual output, which are mirrored by changes in

Forget the pound, the most serious 'P' word for British industry is its failure to lift productivity. For all the talk of a strong pound hitting manufacturers, industrialists face a far more deep-rooted and enduring problem than a temporary lack of a competitive exchange rate. And this one is largely of their own making.

The UK's labour productivity remains at a lamentably low level – around 20 to 30 per cent behind France and Germany and 40 per cent behind the US, according to the latest government figures.

The Confederation of British Industry has calculated that if UK manufacturers could only perform as well as their leading competitors, GDP would increase by £60bn a year, or £3,000 per person.

It is no surprise, then, that Chancellor Gordon Brown has now thrust the 'P' word to the centre stage of economic policy.

Gone are the days when blame for poor workforce performance can be laid at the door of lazy employees and hardline unions – the Thatcher years saw to that. The Eighties saw some improvements, but much was based on longer hours, rather than increased efficiency. British workers now work 9 per cent more hours than German workers, and 5 per cent more than the French, yet our productivity is still below par. Why? A relatively low-skilled and poorly educated workforce combined with a poor record of investment in technology, equipment and infrastructure are seen as culprits. The UK still has the lowest level of investment as a share of national income of all the G7 countries. These long-term problems cannot be solved by quick fixes.

The UK does have its success stories. Its chemical companies are the most productive of all the industrialised nations, and the UK's paper products and printing are second only to the US's. Aerospace companies are also world beaters. But the star performers are few and far between.

Antony Barnett, adapted from 'Work hard, pay hard leaves UK off the pace', *The Observer*, 3 May 1998 unemployment – with unemployment falling at times of above average economic growth and vice versa – tell us very little about changes in the fundamental strength of the supply-side.

Labour productivity

A composite guide to the vitality of the supply-side is the rate of growth of **labour productivity**. Labour productivity measures the output per worker – that is, total output divided by total employment. We know that output can be increased by reducing unemployment, but unless productivity is also raised, such gains do not indicate any sustainable improvement in the supply-side of the economy. Output per head, therefore, offers a guide to the performance of the supply-side, by effectively 'adjusting' increases in output for any change in the level of unemployment.

Although labour productivity gives a better picture of the trends in the underlying developments in the supply-side, its behaviour is, unfortunately, also sensitive to the effects of the economic cycle. In the early stages of a **recession**, firms may be unsure how long the downturn will last and typically 'hoard' their best workers, choosing to cut output and temporarily pay staff in excess of their marginal revenue product in order to avoid the costs of firing and subsequently rehiring workers when business picks up. As a result, output growth falls, but unemployment initially rises only slightly, so that the early stages of the downturn are characterised by a slowdown in productivity growth. At the **trough** of the recession, however, firms are forced to reassess their prospects and lay off workers in order to cut costs. In the middle stages of the recession, therefore, while output growth may not slow any further, unemployment will begin to rise rapidly and the productivity of those employees that remain in work rises.

As **recovery** begins to gather pace, firms expand output by using their existing workforces more intensively – for example, by working staff overtime – waiting to be sure that the upturn will be sustained. Output growth accordingly picks up, but with unemployment little affected, productivity growth accelerates further. Only once the recovery is in full swing and firms start taking on additional staff, does unemployment begin to fall. As the economy approaches the **peak** of the boom, productivity growth gradually slows. Figure 4 illustrates the course of output, unemployment and productivity over the four stages of the economic cycle: recession, trough, recovery and peak.

Since **unemployment** is simply the difference between the potential labour force and employment, we can highlight the triangular nature of the relationship between output, employment and labour productivity.

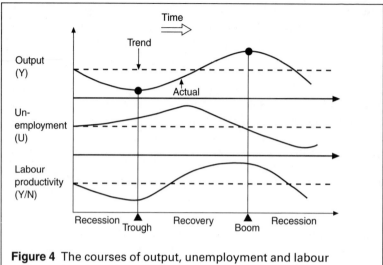

Figure 4 The courses of output, unemployment and labour productivity

Productivity = output/employment

Output = productivity x employment

Output growth (per cent) = productivity growth + employment growth (per cent)

If the potential labour force is unchanged over time (as it is in many European economies, in which the population is fairly static), then in the long run, the growth in labour productivity will be equal to output growth. But in the short run, when employment can fluctuate greatly, output growth can give a misleading impression of the underlying changes in the supply-side, as reflected in changes in productivity. This trinity also illustrates why, in the recovery phase of the economic cycle when productivity normally grows most quickly, unemployment can continue to rise even though output is growing: unless output growth is at least as fast as the growth in productivity, the extra output can be produced with ever fewer workers.

Britain's supply-side performance

Against this background, we can now turn to consider Britain's supply-side performance. Table 2 sets out the performance of the British supply-side over approximately the last 40 years. It shows that, following a period of unprecedented economic growth between 1963 and 1973 – when output (real GDP) grew more rapidly than at any

Table 2 Performance of the British supply-side, 1963–99
(% average annual change, year-on-year)

Years (annual average)	Real GDP	Manuf. output	Labour productivity	Employment	Gross fixed investment
1963–73	3.3	3.6	2.9	0.2	4.8
1973–79	1.5	0.5	1.1	0.2	0.3
1979–95	1.8	0.6	1.8	0.1	2.1
1995–99	3.0	0.4	1.4	1.2	5.2

Sources: Goldman Sachs, Annual Supplements Economic Trends.

time since the Industrial Revolution – the rate of economic growth slowed sharply. The so-called 'long boom' of the 1960s and early 1970s was punctured by the first OPEC oil crisis, when oil prices quadrupled, tipping the world – and Britain – into a deep recession. While growth picked up slightly during the period 1979–95, though dipping during the 1990–92 recession, the improvement was marginal and was partly being constrained during the late 1990s by continental Europe as it prepared itself for monetary union.

Table 2 also shows a change in the performance of the UK economy over the late 1990s and suggests that there is some degree of optimism for the future. Real GDP has returned to levels not seen consistently since the 1960s with anticipated growth in the opening part of the decade to be between 2.75 and 3 per cent. However, both manufacturing productivity and labour productivity, having improved during the period 1979–95, have slipped back indicating that the period of catch-up has stopped. One factor being blamed for this is the lack of highly skilled/educated workers, though lack of appropriate quality investment must also shoulder some of the blame. Employment has grown, partly as a result of a range of measures such as the New Deal brought in to 'encourage' workers back into the job market. In addition there has been a growth in part-time female employment and other types of flexible working arrangements. Gross investment has also picked up, partly as a result of organisational confidence in the consistent macroeconomic policies being followed during the late 1990s. It may also be explained through the growth of '**entrepreneurism**' in the UK economy and via the role and influence of Foreign Direct Investment (FDI).

Structural change

Against this background structural change continues to take place in the UK economy. Manufacturing now constitutes only about 20 per cent of total GDP. (Services account for 70 per cent of total output.) Nonetheless, it continues to generate over half of Britain's export revenues and its vitality is seen as crucial to the nation's economic success – as Germany and Japan have graphically illustrated. Manufacturing in the UK has been on somewhat of a 'roller-coaster ride'. Output from manufacturing rose on average at around 3 per cent annually between 1964 and 1973. However, between 1973 and 1979 output fell and declined even further between 1979 and 1981 (14.2 per cent). By 1990, although manufacturing output had increased it was only 5.4 points above the peak of 1973. The recession in 1991/2 reduced manufacturing output so that by 1997 it was only 10.2 per cent above the level reached in 1973. Thus over the whole period manufacturing output has virtually stagnated.

Labour productivity growth has also fallen sharply since the long boom. Although the period 1973–79 recorded a dismal 1.1 per cent per annum growth in productivity, the improvement since then has been patchy. In the mid-1980s, productivity rattled along at well above 3 per cent per annum, encouraging some commentators to conclude that the 1970s had been a temporary departure from long-term trends. But once the recessions of the 1980–81 and 1990–91 are taken into account, the underlying trend for the period 1979–99 is not as good as might be expected. During this period, labour productivity in Britain was better than that in the US but has lagged behind the annual growth rates achieved by Germany, France and Japan. However, percentage changes in productivity in the case above use different starting levels. If absolute levels are used for the whole UK economy, labour productivity has improved relative to the US since the 1950s. From being over 80 per cent less productive in comparison with the US, the gap had shrunk to around 20 per cent by the late 1990s. With France and Germany, the relative picture is different. The UK had superior productivity in 1950 but by the late 1990s was around 30 per cent less productive than both countries with the gap not appearing to close.

Employment growth

Interestingly, Table 2 shows that employment has grown slowly, but steadily, over the last 40 years. This apparently contradicts the widespread impression that unemployment has been on a relentless upward trend since the mid-1960s. In fact, a combination of demographic and social trends has meant that both rising employment *and* unemployment have occurred simultaneously. During the 1980s and early 1990s while the underlying demand for labour has been continuously expanding, at the same time the supply of labour has grown even more rapidly: more and more young mothers now work; structural changes in working patterns mean that women who would previously have chosen to stay at home can work part-time. By the mid-1990s expansion of both further and higher education, the shift to more flexible patterns of work together with a range of government programmes to encourage people back to work has resulted in the gap between the labour force and employment narrowing. Although it should be noted that the gap is based on claimant figures rather than those actually unemployed.

Finally, the growth in investment by the UK has been rather disappointing. It virtually stagnated during the period 1973–79, it actually grew rather more rapidly than output (implying that the proportion of GDP invested has risen) between 1979 and 1995 and continued to do so during 1995–99. Nevertheless, although Britain enjoyed something of an investment boom during the late 1980s and the second half of the 1990s, the increase in the total capital stock since 1979 is disappointingly small. Indeed, the capital stock levels differ by sectors, within sectors, and in relation to other countries. By the late 1990s, the UK appeared to have narrowed the gap between level of capital per hour worked between itself and the US (though the US was still 31 per cent ahead). In comparison in France, Germany and Japan the capital intensity gaps have widened to 36 per cent, 55 per cent and 40 per cent respectively. Let us look at these international comparisons in more detail.

International comparisons

Table 3 compares Britain's supply-side performance since the end of the long boom with its main partners in the European Union. It shows that on nearly every indicator, Britain ranks last amongst the 'big four':

- GDP and labour productivity growth rates have been slower.
- Relative **unit labour costs**[1] have increased more rapidly.
- Employment growth has been more sluggish.
- Only gross domestic fixed capital formation has grown more quickly.

Although some of the differences appear small, it is important to bear in mind the effect of compounding. For example, over the twenty-one

Table 3 Relative performance of the British supply-side,
1974–99 (% average annual changes year-on-year)

	Real GDP	Labour productivity*	Relative unit labour costs[1]*	Employment	Gross fixed investment
Britain	2.06	1.71	1.97	0.22	2.02
Germany	2.10	1.93	−0.80	0.27	2.29
France	2.25	1.94	−0.25	0.28	1.43
Italy	2.48	1.86	0.41	0.55	1.49

[1]Relative to other EU member states (see also note 1).
*1974–98.
Source: *European Economy*.

years between 1974 and 1995, the extra 0.3 per cent GDP growth
enjoyed by France meant that, had Britain and France had the same
GDP in 1973, by 1995 the French GDP would be over 6 per cent
higher (in fact, French GDP was already well above British GDP in
1973, so the gap was even greater).

Although Table 3 provides us with the long-term trends for a number of major economic indicators, more recent performances will tend
to get absorbed in the figures. Thus if Britain's growth rates or labour
productivity has improved it will take a long time for any catch-up to
show itself in the long-term trend figures. Table 4 seeks to address this
issue. It should be noted that short-term changes may not be representative of long-run effects but Table 4 does give some reason to be more

Table 4 Relative performance of the British supply-side,
1996–99 (% average annual changes year-on-year)

	Real GDP	Labour productivity*	Relative unit labour costs[1]*	Employment	Gross fixed investment
Britain	2.6	1.25	9.43	0.93	4.73
Germany	2.6	2.63	−5.27	−0.18	5.80
France	2.5	1.65	−2.07	0.70	2.63
Italy	1.9	1.15	4.83	0.28	4.08

[1]Relative to other EU member states (see also note 1).
*1996–98.
Source: *European Economy*.

optimistic with the UK's performance. The UK's real GDP per head now matches that of its major European rivals, labour productivity growth rates have improved, employment prospects have improved as has gross fixed capital investment. Nonetheless, real unit labour costs still lie above its major rivals.

The future for Britain's supply-side performance

Although there is some evidence that Britain's economic performance had begun to improve in 1998, productivity in terms of output per worker still shows a gap of up to a third with countries like the US, France and Germany. However, the picture changes if we consider output per hour, with France and Germany 30 per cent higher than the UK and the US only 20 per cent ahead. If we measure productivity in terms of total factor productivity (a measure of the efficiency of both capital and labour), then this is almost 20 per cent higher in France but only around 10 per cent higher in Germany and the US. In fact the picture becomes further complicated if we take GDP per head. In 1997 the OECD found that France was only 3 per cent ahead of the UK, Germany 8 per cent per cent on the same measure, but the US 40 per cent greater. Why the differences in rankings? It is partly explained by the greater proportion of people in the 15–64 age group who are in work. Seventy-one per cent of the British people in this age group and 74 per cent of US citizens were in employment; this compares with 59 per cent of the French and 64 per cent of the Germans. Flexible labour and capital markets manifest themselves in low labour productivity or output per head. Germany and France, with less flexible labour and capital markets, have lower employment and higher joblessness. In addition the wide productivity gap figures can also be misleading. They result partly from ignoring the so-called non-market sector such as government services, health and education.

After large improvements in Britain's productivity performance during the late 1980s and 1990s, closing the gap with its major competitors has become more difficult due to skill deficiencies, investment issues and skill shortages. The UK Paper on **Competitiveness** (1999) pointed to the importance of the knowledge-based economy (see Chapter 7), and the fact that Britain faces several longstanding shortcomings diminishing its international competitiveness:

- the failure to match the performance of overseas competitors in productivity, innovation and quality;
- under-investment in physical assets but also in R&D and other tangible assets;
- low skill levels.

Government responses to supply-side constraints

The McKinsey Global Institute in their competitiveness report on the UK (1999) also pointed to the excessive regulatory burden faced by UK companies and insufficient competition as two of the main causes of the productivity gap between UK companies and their US rivals. McKinsey argue that, if these constraints were removed, Britain's growth rate could average 3.5 per cent per annum instead of around 2 per cent and this would allow the UK to reach existing levels of US gross domestic product per head within ten years. Moreover, it is argued that UK management often fails to adopt global best practices even when in some cases these are readily understandable and achievable and this is far more important than vocational training in generating higher productivity.

The government has noted these constraints and in order to achieve the improvement in the supply-side, the government, in their Competitiveness Paper (1999), have set out a number of competitiveness indicators to measure the UK's progress in meeting the challenges of the knowledge economy and to close the performance gap with other advanced economies. The 39 indicators are grouped under four main headings working from the business environment and inputs, through processes to results:

- the business environment – measures of macroeconomic stability, competition, business perceptions and the quality of life in the UK;
- resources – measures of human and physical capital, finance, technology and R&D;
- innovation process – measures of commercial exploitation of science and technology, entrepreneurship, diffusion of knowledge across borders and between firms; and
- results – GDP per head, productivity, employment and trade, and the changing nature of output.

The following chapters examine Britain's performance in these areas.

Conclusions

Supply-side performance is often taken to be synonymous with economic growth – that is, the rate of change of output. In fact, the rate of growth of output is highly cyclical, typically accelerating during an economic upswing and slowing during recession. It can therefore be misleading to try and infer what is happening to the underlying rate of economic growth from the rate of change of output over a relatively short period. Measuring output growth from peak to peak (ie, from the peak of one cycle to the peak of the next) gives a better impression of trends on the supply-side, but since no two economic cycles are precisely the same, even this approach has important limitations.

Bearing these caveats in mind, over the long run, Britain's supply-side performance does appear to suggest that other countries do not have far greater problems than we have. While output has grown at an average rate of approximately 2 per cent per annum over the last 30 years, approximately doubling real living standards over this period, in comparison with other developed countries Britain has fared badly. Second only to the United States in terms of per capita income in 1960, Britain has steadily slipped down the international league table, as Japan and almost all of the northern European states have overtaken it. Have the policy changes begun in the 1980s worked? It is to a better understanding of both past and current supply-side policies that we now turn.

KEY WORDS

Natural rate of output	Peak
Stop-go	Unemployment
Labour productivity	Entrepreneurism
Recession	Unit labour costs
Trough	Competitiveness
Recovery	

Further reading

Bamford, C. and Grant, S. (2000), Chapter 3 in, *The UK Economy in a Global Context*, Studies in Economics and Business, Heinemann Educational.

Bazen, S. and Thirlwall, T. (1996), *Deindustrialization*, 3rd edn, Heinemann Educational.

Cook, M. and Healey, N. (1995), *Growth and Structural Change*, Macmillan.

Grant, S. (1999), Chapters 1 and 2 in, *Economics and Business Cycles*, Studies in Economics and Business, Heinemann.

Smith, D. (1999), Chapters 6 and 7 in, *UK Current Economic Policy*, 2nd edn, Studies in Economics and Business, Heinemann.

Useful websites

Organisation for Economic Co-operation and Development: http://www.oecd.org/

DFP Economics Branches: http://www.dfpni.gov.UK/economics_division/reports/quarterly
Department of Trade and Industry: http://www.dti.gov.UK/

Notes

1. Unit labour costs = $\dfrac{\text{wage} + \text{non-wage costs per worker}}{\text{average product per worker}}$

Unit labour costs therefore rise when wage or non-wage (eg, employers' national insurance contributions) increase and fall as productivity rises.

Relative unit labour costs (RULCs) are unit labour costs expressed in a common currency and related to the average of a group of countries (in Table 2, the EU as a whole). A rise in RULCs implies deteriorating competitiveness, which could stem from a relative increase in wage or non-wage costs, in domestic currency terms; a relative decline in the growth of labour productivity; or an appreciation in the exchange rate. Conversely, a fall in RULCs implies increasing competitiveness.

Chapter Two

The determinants of supply-side performance

'Too many of our workforce, raised in the routine "jobs for life" culture of the 1950s, 60s and 70s, left school with few qualifications if any. They lack the basic skills, aspiration, self-belief – and frequently the opportunity – to broaden their horizons through the power of learning.' Third Report of the National Skills Task Force, 2000

Introduction

Although we are interested in what determines the supply-side performance of the economy, the supply-side of the economy and economic growth are interdependent. The factors that determine economic growth such as quantity and quality of labour and capital, and quantity and quality of technology (total factor productivity), can be influenced by supply-side policy by not only considering research and development, and investment but also focusing on education and training, industrial organisation, working practices and a whole range of further incentives that optimises usage of any new techniques that are introduced.

The economy typically moves in a cyclical fashion, with output and unemployment fluctuating over time. These fluctuations can be broadly explained by reference to the behaviour of AD in the AS–AD model in Figure 5.

The economic cycle and changes in aggregate demand

Suppose that AD begins to increase from AD_0. In the short run, money illusion persists and the economy slides up $SRAS(P_0)$. Firms find output and profits rising, encouraging them to invest in additional capacity; households enjoy rising incomes, inducing them to borrow more and increase current consumption in the expectation of even higher incomes tomorrow. As corporate and consumer confidence rises, the increase in AD becomes self-fuelling, eventually pushing it out to AD_1. At this point, the economy has experienced a sharp increase in real output, from Y_0 to Y_1, at the cost of only a modest increase in prices (ie, inflation) from P_0 to P_1.

Gradually, however, bottlenecks emerge on the supply-side. Skill shortages develop in the labour market. And, with the demand for

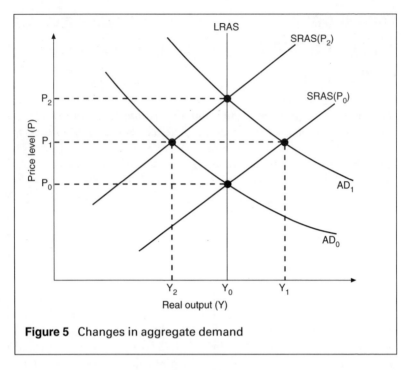

Figure 5 Changes in aggregate demand

labour strong, as workers begin to realise that inflation is undermining the real value of their wages, unions start to bid aggressively for higher wages. As money illusion fades, the SRAS schedule drifts to the left. A destructive **wage-price spiral** is set in motion as the boom peaks, with the leftwards shift in the SRAS schedule from $SRAS(P_0)$ towards $SRAS(P_2)$ causing output to fall and prices to rise higher still. As profits and output fall, firms cut back investment plans; consumer confidence collapses; and AD shifts leftwards, from AD_1 towards AD_0. Instead of reaching a new long-run equilibrium at P_2, Y_0, the economy instead moves into recession, with output falling below the natural rate, Y_0, to Y_2, until prices and wages adjust sufficiently for confidence and spending to increase once more and set the cycle off again.

It is clear from this account that the original increase in output from Y_0 to Y_1 is not economic growth; nor is the subsequent fall in output from Y_1 to Y_2 a contraction in the economy's supply-side potential. Both are simply the results of the fluctuations in AD that appear to characterise free market economies. In contrast, economic growth implies a sustained increase in the economy's capacity to produce real goods and services in the long run, independent of changes in AD (and unemployment); that is, a rightward shift in the LRAS schedule.

Economic growth and the long-run aggregate supply schedule

Economic growth thus means a rightwards shift in the LRAS – for example, from $LRAS_0$ to $LRAS_1$ in Figure 6a. At $LRAS_1$, the economy can enjoy more goods and services at any given price level. How could such an increase in the underlying or long-run level of real output come about? First, consider the labour market in Figure 6b. If the labour supply were to increase – either because there was an increase in the number of workers available for employment or because the existing workforce offered more hours' labour at any given money

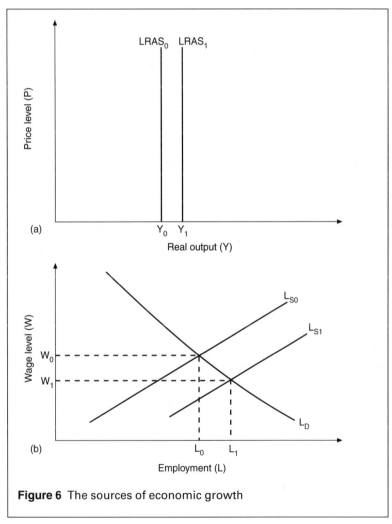

Figure 6 The sources of economic growth

wage – this would shift the labour supply schedule to the right from L_{S0} to L_{S1}, raising equilibrium employment from L_0 to L_1. This could be aided if:

- the productivity of labour were to rise, because the 'quality' of labour was increased through better training and education;
- the capital stock were to rise, allowing each employee to produce more output for a given number of hours worked; or
- technological advances were to improve the 'quality' of the capital stock, enabling each worker to produce more output from a given amount of machinery.

Growth theories compared

Given that growth and productivity are seen as providing increases in real incomes whilst allowing a redistribution of income to take place without the need to resort to the burden of taxation, what is required is some understanding of the determinants of growth. Once these are understood then supply-side policies can be used to stimulate the explanatory variable behind the growth process.

Theories of growth fall into two main areas, **neo-classical growth models** and **endogenous growth models**. In the neo-classical growth models, growth is determined by the amount of capital and labour available, but technology or technical progress is outside of the control of governments. In other words it is exogenous. Thus we have:

$$Y = Af\,(L,K)$$

where, L = labour input; K = capital input; A = technical progress; and Y = output.

Changes in output would therefore come about from changes in the labour input – determined by changes in the level of working population, or changes in the level of capital stimulated through the availability of savings. However, if the quantity of labour is relatively fixed, then increasing the amount of savings for investment purposes would lead to diminishing returns to capital. Thus increasing savings would not lead to long-term improvements in growth rather just to short-term spurts. In addition, because technology is available to all in the long term, what we should see is growth rates converging. Besides, for countries with low capital/labour ratios, there should be a high marginal productivity of capital and they should be better able to attract foreign capital to invest in equipment which may in itself embody technical progress. In reality when studies were undertaken on various countries, growth rates did not appear to be reducing over time, in fact the reverse appeared to be happening. Furthermore, A (technical progress) appeared to be explaining the greater part of any variation in growth rates between countries.

As an attempt to explain why technical progress was important in growth, theories were put forward which attempted to endogenise it. In other words a range of factors were put forward which could explain the size and variation over time of technical progress or total factor productivity. The factors included:

- quality and quantity of investment in human resources involving amount of schooling, education and training
- the amount and quality of investment and R&D
- economic stability through low and consistent inflation rates
- reductions in government expenditure as part of total expenditure
- openness to trade and foreign direct investment.

During the 40 years from 1960–1999, real output has grown at an average, year-on-year rate of 2–3 per cent. Table 5 indicates the performance of the UK relative to its major competitors.

Over this time, the average number of hours worked each week has fallen steadily, partly as a result of the European **Working Time Directive,** while more and more young people have stayed on in school and older workers have retired earlier. Although there have been trends in the opposite direction, most notably an increase in the population and a rise in the proportion of married women working, the growth in the labour force from 25 million in 1979 to 28.5 million in 1998 can account for only a proportion of the overall increase in output over the last hundred years.

The primary source of the increase in our living standards has been better training and education, capital investment and R&D, rather than ever harder work. It is to a consideration of Britain's record in each of these three areas that we now turn.

Table 5 Average annual growth in GDP, G7 countries, 1960–99

	1960–67	1968–73	1974–79	1980–89	1990–99
USA	4.5	3.2	2.4	2.5	2.7
Japan	10.2	8.7	3.6	4.0	1.5
Germany	4.1	4.9	2.3	1.8	2.4
France	5.4	5.5	2.8	2.2	1.8
UK	3.0	3.4	1.5	2.4	1.8
Italy	5.7	4.5	3.7	2.4	1.3
Canada	5.5	5.4	4.2	3.1	2.0
Average G7	5.0	4.4	2.7	2.8	1.9

Source: OECD, Economic Outlook 1999.

Training and education

The British system of training and education has long been regarded as a root cause of the economy's poor productivity record. On almost all measures of human capital acquisition, Britain compares unfavourably with the other major economies in Europe and in comparison with both the US and Japan the picture is even worse. Britain has a relatively low proportion of 16–24 year olds in further education and the least educated managerial class in Europe.

The real problem is not with higher levels of qualification but with the supply of qualified young people with craft-related vocational qualifications (Levels 2 and 3). This comparison between France and Germany is particularly pronounced in relation to 25–28 year olds. The result is that employers are often employing graduates in the absence of applicants with technician and associated professional qualifications, and this has in part contributed to complaints from employers that graduate recruits have inadequate technical and commercial skills. The picture is also made worse when we examine older age groups. Most of the growth in qualifications over the last 20 years has been generated by new entrants to the labour market, not by adult upskilling. Thus the likelihood of holding any formal qualification falls dramatically by age. A 40–49 year old is more than twice as likely to possess no formal qualification compared with a 20–29 year old and a 50–59 year old is almost 4 times as likely to possess none.

Level of training

One aspect often related to the UK's flexible labour market is that the UK will under-invest in skill training for its workforce. This low level of training by companies is believed to stem from the nature of the British labour market, in which workers expect to move jobs frequently – in contrast to Japan, for example, where workers often stay with the same employer throughout their working lives. This mobility reduces the incentive for firms to train their staff. Rather than expensively training workers who may then move to rival firms, it is more cost-effective for each firm to 'free-ride', waiting for others to pay for training and then 'poaching' trained staff by paying marginally higher wages. The result is that, at an economy-wide level, there is a tendency for British firms to collectively under-train staff, damaging their longer-term competitiveness. However, a survey undertaken in 1993 suggests that training activity in the UK is broadly comparable to that in other European countries. When the type of training is examined, a larger share of the provision recorded in the UK was accounted for by *job and environment* training – around a third in UK manufacturing compared with 5–10 per cent in Germany and France. Training in *production techniques* was much lower in the UK at around 8 per cent compared with the 25 per cent in Germany and 45 per cent in France.

Although there is evidence that **skills gaps** have reduced in the UK workforce the decline in the skills gap associated with their current workforce has been replaced with a skills gap associated with recruitment. In other words, there are still problems with filling vacancies. The National Skills Task Force noted in 2000 that the skills needs for industry covered a number of areas:

- basic skills – those associated with literacy and numeracy;
- generic skills – those transferable skills, essential for employability;
- mathematical skills – poor supply and increasing demand for these skills;
- intermediate level skills – specific occupational skills needed in intermediate jobs ranging from craft to associated professional occupations, ie, Levels 3 and 4;
- specialist information and communication technology skills
- major adult skill gaps – large proportion of the adult workforce with no qualifications or qualifications below Level 2.

Capital investment

Expressed as a percentage of GDP, capital investment in Britain falls well below the levels enjoyed in Germany and Japan. These decades of underinvestment are estimated to show that capital stock available per hour worked in the market sector in 1999 (ie, excluding the health, education and government sectors) were 13 per cent higher in Japan, 19 per cent higher in the US, 33 per cent higher in France and 40 per cent higher in Germany. The continuing failure of British firms to invest as heavily as their overseas rivals, despite the removal of allegedly restrictive taxes and government regulations, suggests that there may be inherent deficiencies in the way that the private sector functions. For example, critics point to the structure of the British capital market, which – in contrast to those in Germany and Japan – allows companies that do not maximise short-term profits to be taken over against their will. As a result, British management may be deterred from undertaking the investment essential for longer-term economic success, since payback periods are typically long so that investment reduces profits in the short term. In addition, we could point to the lack of well-developed **venture capital markets**, lack of sizeable vibrant markets in which entrepreneurs can float their companies and sell their shares, and failure to develop an entrepreneurial spirit and risk-taking attitude that exists in the US. Fiscal incentives – for example, tax allowances or capital grants – may be necessary, it is argued, to induce

Gordon Brown has made his intentions clear. The left had got it wrong by concentrating on the good society at the expense of the good economy, while the right had championed the good economy and forgotten all about the good society. His goal, he said, was to secure fairness and enterprise at the same time.

It is a mark of how far Labour has moved in the past decade that a Labour chancellor would be talking of daily signing-on for benefit claimants and cutting capital gains tax for entrepreneurs.

Much of the language used by Labour has a Thatcherite feel to it, almost as if Brown was holding out the prospect of trickle-down, Labour fashion, with the wealth generated by a new generation of hi-tech entrepreneurs cascading down the income scale. Brown and his advisers argue that the strategy will deliver, over the long term, the sort of enterprising yet inclusive society they are seeking.

The four key areas for action are: first, the reforms of monetary and fiscal policy are a necessary but not sufficient factor for higher levels of growth. Britain has a lower level of productivity than other leading industrial countries, so he is looking to the cuts in capital gains tax, investment allowances and tougher competition policy to produce faster growth in output per head.

Although increasing physical investment and developing the new sunrise industries is seen as vital, the chancellor says that the seven million adults lacking basic skills in literacy and numeracy means that the UK is deficient when it comes to human capital. The second aim for the next decade, therefore, is to ensure that a majority of school-leavers go on to degrees.

The third leg of the Brown strategy has been evident from Day 1 of the Blair administration: the emphasis on work. With long-term unemployment falling and £570 million unspent from the windfall levy on the privatised utilities, the government can now afford to extend the New Deal to all workers over 25 who have been out of work for more than a year. The chancellor said his aim over 10 years was to achieve a higher percentage of people in work than ever before.

Finally, there is child poverty. Boosting productivity, increasing the number of people in work and at the same time working smarter will, the chancellor believes, allow him to meet the fourth objective, cutting the number of children in poverty by half over the next decade.

Larry Elliott, Economics Editor, adapted from 'Chancellor taking the American Democrat route', *The Guardian*, 10 November 1999

firms to spend on R&D and invest in physical capital in such circumstances.

Conclusions

In this chapter, we have seen that economic growth is a supply-side phenomenon. In terms of the AS–AD model, it refers to a rightward shift in the LRAS schedule; that is, an increase in the natural rate of output. Whether exogenous growth or endogenous growth models explain growth performances better, there is some commonalty as to what underlies the growth process: improved investment in schooling, education and skills; the quality and quantity of savings and investment; the level of human capital, and stability of the economy. Growth reducing factors include: high levels of government consumption spending; political and social instability; trade barriers, and historically the association of some political parties with particular doctrines.

But where economists have failed to provide a clear lead is in identifying the factors that influence each of these driving forces that underpin economic growth.

- How does the tax and social security system affect the labour supply?
- Is the best way of stimulating private sector investment in human and physical capital an unregulated, *laissez-faire* environment?
- Is activist demand management necessary to guarantee firms a healthy, growing market for the output and thereby encourage investment and risk-taking?
- What is the role for fiscal incentives (eg, tax allowances, public subsidies) to promote investment and R&D?

Economists have produced no clear-cut answers to these critical questions. The following chapters will explore the basic theoretical differences and the out-turns of the policies between those who argue that government intervention is necessary for a strong supply-side, and those who argue for a deregulated, liberalised economy in which the free market can operate unhindered.

KEY WORDS

Wage-price spiral	Working Time Directive
Economic growth	Free-ride
Neo-classical growth models	Skills gaps
Endogenous growth models	Venture capital markets

Further reading

Al-Ubaydii, O. and Kealey, T. (2000), 'Endogenous growth theory: a critique', *Economic Affairs*, September, pp. 10–13.

Backhouse, R. (2000), 'How can governments deal with the problem of labour market failure?', *Economics Today*, Vol. 7, No. 3, pp. 28–31.

Cook, M. (1996), 'Economic growth and the UK economy', *Economics and Business Education*, Vol. IV, Part 2, No. 14, pp. 52–57.

Cook, M. and Healey, N. (1995), *Growth and Structural Change*, Macmillan.

Useful websites
EU official website: www.europa.eu.int/en/comm/eurostat/
DFEE: www.dfee.gov.uk/
Manchester Information and Associated Services (MIMAS): www.mimas.ac.uk/

Essay topics
1. (a) Explain how supply-side policies might be used to:
   (i) reduce the level of unemployment;
   (ii) increase the rate of economic growth. [70 marks]
   (b) To what extent have supply-side policies been effective in achieving these aims in the UK? [30 marks]
   [Edexcel, Paper 2, Q8, June 1996].

2. (a) How might supply-side policies help to increase the country's rate of economic growth? [50 marks]
   (b) Evaluate the possible benefits and costs of a faster rate of economic growth in a country of your choice. [50 marks]
   [Edexcel, Paper 2, Q8, June 1998].

Data response question
The following task is based on a question set by OCR in 2000.

A National Minimum Wage

In May 1998, the Government-appointed Low Pay Commission (LPC) produced its first report. Amongst its recommendations was that there should be a National Minimum Wage (NMW) of £3.60 per hour.

The introduction of a NMW in the UK is argued by the LPC to be 'a major
5 initiative to address **in-work poverty** and promote **work incentives**. It should also bring a range of further benefits, including greater equality in pay between the sexes and between people of different ethnic backgrounds. There are also advantages for business and the wider community. By promoting greater fairness, it will encourage employee commitment, reduce
10 staff turnover, and act as a spur to productivity and competitiveness.

It is acknowledged that criticism exists about the introduction of a NMW, especially in the areas of:

- **pay differentials**
- business costs
15 • competitiveness
- prices
- employment
- public sector finances.

However, the LPC has surveyed the experience of many other countries
20 which have introduced a NMW, and offers the following two conclusions:
'On the **pay differentials** aspect, almost all studies find that a NMW
does lead to a compression of the earnings distribution i.e. the pressure to restore **pay differentials** is limited.'
'Sensibly set minimum wages have contributed successfully to
25 social policy without a significant adverse effect on employment.'

Source: Labour Market Trends, September 1998

1. (a) Define **each** of the following terms and state how, **in each case,**
   it might be affected by the National Minimum Wage (NMW):
   (i)   in-work poverty (line 5)   [2 marks]
   (ii) work incentives (line 5)   [2 marks]
   (iii) pay differentials (lines 21–3).   [2 marks]

   (b) Explain why the introduction of 'sensibly set minimum wages'
   may **not** have a 'significant adverse effect on employment'
   (lines 24–5).   [4 marks]

   (c) Explain why the LPC might believe that the introduction of
   a NMW should bring 'greater equality in pay between the
   sexes and between people of different ethnic backgrounds'
   (lines 6–7).   [2 marks]

   (d) Discuss the possible effects of the introduction of a NMW both
   on the distribution of income **and** on the competitiveness of the
   British economy.   [8 marks]

Chapter Three

An overview of British supply-side policies, 1945 to the present

'Mr Brown is neither a monetarist nor a Keynesian – but something called a post-monetarist. He ... who has Keynesian objectives – but believes in using monetarist means to achieve them.'
Larry Elliott, October 1999

Introduction

Ten years ago the two pivotal approaches to improving the performance of the UK economy could be seen within the Keynesian and new classical schools of thought. Both offered almost diametrically opposed approaches as to how growth and productivity should be improved. In the former, the idea was that market failure existed and that the private sector, if left to its own devices, would under-invest in the economy and that some form of government involvement or planning was required if growth and productivity were to be improved. The new classical school turned these ideas on their head. In their view, the market mechanism worked very efficiently and the reason why growth and productivity have been disappointing is because the government is far too active in the market place and that market forces should be introduced into solving the demand and supply for products and services. An historic view would be to associate the Keynesian view with Labour and the new classical view with Conservatism.

All this has changed during the late 1990s. New Labour espouses both the ideas of using incentives, low taxes, free movements of capital and more self-reliance whilst at the same time having a role for the government of economic stability, controlling the abuse of market power and providing support for individuals. The ideas of the knowledge economy, innovation and entrepreneurship are words frequently used as targets over the last few years. In other words we have supply-siders and those who believe in demand management rather than left or right political party dogma.

The traditional Keynesian view of the supply-side

Until the end of the 1970s, macroeconomic policy in Britain reflected an essentially **'Keynesian view'** of the way the economy operated.

Keynesian economists believed that, in terms of the aggregate supply and demand (AS–AD):

- the private sector components of aggregate demand were very unstable, so that total spending would tend to fluctuate unpredictably in the absence of government intervention; and
- the responsiveness of wages to changes in the price level – particularly in a downward direction – was very slow.

In particular, Keynesians were concerned that, left to its own devices, aggregate demand might fall, causing the economy to operate below its natural rate of output for extended periods. With wages 'sticky' **downwards**, rather than wages falling to clear the labour market and – by allowing firms to pass on the reduction in labour costs in the form of lower prices – pushing the economy back towards its natural rate of output, the economy would instead suffer persistent unemployment. Keynesians also recognised that spontaneous increases in aggregate demand might equally well lead to inflation, as output increased above its natural rate, but they tended to regard the possibility of unemployment as the greater danger.

Keynesians accordingly recommended that governments should aim to stabilise the level of aggregate demand at the natural rate of output, neutralising fluctuations in the private sector components of spending by appropriate adjustments in government spending, tax rates and interest rates. **Discretionary fiscal and monetary policy** of this type is normally referred to as 'fine-tuning'. Not only was this approach to demand management policy urged as the only way of avoiding the twin ills of unemployment and inflation, but Keynesians also argued that stabilising aggregate demand was the best way to promote economic growth. Because investment in R&D and physical and human capital is so sensitive to expectations about the future level of demand for firms' finished products, Keynesians claimed that only by ensuring a high, stable level of aggregate demand would firms be able to enjoy the confidence they needed to invest for the future.

This view of the world was based on the proposition that the unbridled operation of free markets would fail to propel the economy efficiently towards its natural rate of output and unemployment following changes in aggregate demand. Consistent with this, Keynesians argued that government intervention in the supply-side was also essential if countries were to maximise their growth potential.

Market failure and externalities
How do considerations of externalities relate to the supply-side?

31

Keynesians argue that many of the key determinants of economic growth are plagued by **positive externalities**, so that the free market will tend to under-invest in R&D and physical and human capital. As a result, the growth rate will be slower than socially optimal. Given the presence of positive externalities, Keynesians argued, the amount of R&D undertaken by firms in aggregate is likely to be **socially sub-optimal**, with many firms preferring to wait for their rivals to make the technological breakthroughs. It is significant that, in Japan, where the corporate system of '*keiretzu*' ties together otherwise independent companies through a complex series of interlocking directorships and shareholdings, companies do not have the same incentive to free-ride on the R&D of others and Japan is a clearly established world leader in high-tech industries. In Britain, on the other hand, Keynesians concluded that the same effect could only be achieved through government intervention.

Training and education may also be subject to similar effects. Imagine that in the absence of publicly-provided training and education, a private company decides to offer training services to subscribing firms. While each firm would pay to send its staff on the training courses, each guesses (rightly) that, by not paying, the benefits can be enjoyed by 'free-riding' at their neighbours' expense, since they may be able to poach trained workers from their rivals by paying only slightly above the present market wage. As a result, many firms refuse to subscribe and the ensuing service is socially sub-optimal. An alternative solution would be to provide the training publicly, financing it with a tax which each company will willingly pay, in the knowledge that the scheme constrains their neighbours to join with them in a collectively advantageous enterprise.

Information and economic coordination

Just as Keynesians were sceptical about the ability of free markets to keep the economy at its natural rates of output and unemployment over time, so they believed that the 'invisible hand' was ill suited to the task of coordinating investment across a modern economy. How was each stage of a production process that might lead to a final physical output or service supposed to have sufficient knowledge of the demands and desires of other stages in the production process? Keynesians argued that this was not possible and concluded that the invisible hand was therefore likely to be incapable of coordinating the investment decisions across the economy in a way that would maximise the rate of economic growth. While the guarantee of high and stable levels of aggregate demand would undoubtedly help,

Keynesians argued that governments should play a more explicit role in ensuring balanced growth. This attitude to the functioning of the economy became influential in the early 1960s, following the apparent success of national economic planning in countries as diverse as the former Soviet Union, Japan and France.

The Keynesian supply-side prescription

Persuaded by the Keynesians' diagnosis of Britain's economic ills, during the period 1945–79 successive governments concentrated their supply-side efforts on three main fronts:

- attempts to plan the economy;
- taking firms into public ownership;
- government-directed investment, training and industrial restructuring.

These policies were not without their critics. New classical economists attacked fine-tuning as inflationary and counterproductive, rejecting the notion that the private sector was inherently unstable and claiming that wages adjusted rapidly to changes in prices. More significantly, they also dismissed the proposition that the price mechanism was unable to coordinate economic activity and generate the optimal levels of investment. They claimed instead that Britain's supply-side weaknesses resulted from excessive government interference in the economy, rather than any inherent deficiency in the private sector. They alleged that the growth of the public sector, which took output and employment decisions on non-commercial grounds, and the increase in taxes necessary to finance the welfare state, had seriously damaged the incentives to invest. It is to this critique of the Keynesian era and the policy recommendations of the new classical school that we now turn.

The new classical economists believed that the private sector was inherently efficient, with unfettered labour and goods markets clearing quickly and the economy automatically tending to its natural rate of output. They concluded, moreover, that far from being necessary to stabilise aggregate demand and thereby promote investment and economic growth, discretionary demand management policy had in fact been positively destabilising. For example, if aggregate demand were to fall in Figure 7 from AD_0 to AD_1, the short-run aggregate supply schedule would quickly shift down from $SRAS(P_0)$ to $SRAS(P_2)$, as lower prices fed through into lower wage settlements. If the government responded to the initial contraction in demand by relaxing fiscal and monetary policy, driving aggregate demand back to AD_0, as these

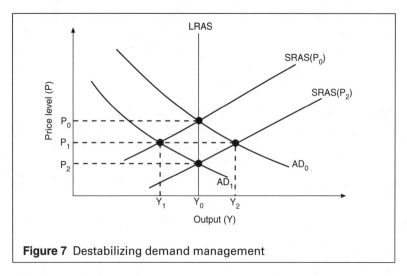

Figure 7 Destabilizing demand management

lagged effects spread through the economy, the economy would slide up its new short-run aggregate supply schedule, $SRAS(P_2)$, throwing the economy back into disequilibrium just as it was recovering from the initial demand-side 'shock'.

Moreover, to the extent that markets did not appear to clear as smoothly as new classical economists claimed, they argued that any sluggishness was due to the interference of government, which had injected damaging distortions into the economic system. Nationalisation, state controls and regulations, and high taxes were singled out for particular criticism in this regard. In contrast to the Keynesians, who had highlighted the importance of market failure as the primary source of supply-side weakness in the British economy, the new classical economists stressed the need to liberate and properly reward individual enterprise.

The rationale of new classical supply-side policies

Like Keynesians, the **new classical school** faced the task of explaining why it is that some countries undertake more R&D and invest more in physical and human capital than others, thereby reaping the benefits of faster economic growth. In providing their answer to this conundrum, the new classical school emphasised the importance of individual economic agents, motivated by self-interest and reacting to the incentives and sanctions provided by the economic system within which they operate. In this, the new classical economists drew upon a long tradition, extending back to Adam Smith's famous book, *The Wealth of Nations* and revitalised by the more recent ideas of **Hayek** and the so-called '**Austrian school**'. The latter stressed the vital function of competitive markets in providing people with the incentives to seek out information about profitable opportunities for production and exchange. Information concerning the most efficient methods of production and which goods are most valued by consumers will only be discovered by economic agents with a personal incentive to do so, because they expect to benefit as a consequence.

The key economic agents on the supply-side of the economy are the various categories of producers – **entrepreneurs**, managers and workers – together with investors (those people who are postponing consumption by investing in productive assets) and their advisers, the financial institutions. According to the new classical view, entrepreneurs are motivated by the expectation of profit to discover and supply products that consumers want and to use efficient production methods. The stimulus to serve consumers is best provided in competitive markets. If there are few rival suppliers to whom consumers can turn if they are dissatisfied, then firms can still earn profits even while operating with costs above the feasible minimum or failing to produce the type and quality of goods consumers prefer. Without the stimulus of competition, a firm has less inducement to organize its workforce efficiently, to provide its employees with incentives to work efficiently and to satisfy customers' wants.

The new classical economists' scepticism about the ability of governments to improve economic performance by means of direct intervention is based on the argument that governments cannot obtain the requisite information about the most efficient ways of allocating resources. The market is more efficient at discovering and transmitting such information because it relies on specialists in particular market niches obtaining and using information about the kinds of goods and services demanded by consumers and about the cheapest methods of production. The economy is also dynamic, in the sense that it continually generates new applications for technical knowledge and adapts rapidly and smoothly to changes in the forces of demand and supply, if, and only if, individual economic agents have the appropriate incentives.

On this view of the world, the role of government is to ensure that the laws, regulations and institutions operate so as to provide economic agents with the required incentives and information. Direct intervention by government is doomed to be inefficient. Governments cannot obtain the requisite information at the right time and are pressured by special interest (or 'rent-seeking') groups to allocate resources to satisfy their own specific interests.

The rationale of new classical supply-side policies is thus derived directly from this view of how markets operate in allocating resources, in contrast to the comparative inefficiency of government regulation. The general aim of new classical supply-side policies is to strengthen and extend competitive market forces and to alter existing laws and regulations in order to improve the incentives for individuals to seek out productive activities. Inspired by the new classical school, the Conservative government that came to power in 1979 rejected the Keynesian supply-side policies that it inherited and introduced a raft of new measures which included:

- privatisation of public enterprises;
- deregulation of the goods and capital markets;
- reform of the tax and social security system to increase incentives to work and invest;
- legislative changes designed to liberalise the labour market;
- reduction in red tape and other impediments to investment and risk taking;
- reduction in government expenditure to release more resources for the private sector;
- encouragement of competition through policies of deregulation and privatisation;
- abolition of exchange controls and other impediments to the free movement of capital;
- increasing share ownership;
- improvements in the skills and training of the labour force;
- development of mass home-ownership.

The Third Way

The entry of New Labour into power in 1997 did not see a return to increased government involvement in the economy in terms of nationalisation and government-directed investment, training and restructuring of the economy, as might have been expected. Instead we saw the development of what has been called the 'Third Way'.

So what has been the general thrust of New Labour's supply-side policies under the Third Way?

- Getting people back to work – through **reskilling** or through job subsidies.
- Ensuring those in work are better paid through the introduction of Working Family Tax Credit, child-care tax credits, the introduction of a minimum wage and lower taxes for the less well-off.
- Measures to boost enterprise and innovation, in particular focusing on high-technology start-ups and small businesses.

As a concept, the Third Way is as slippery as compacted snow on a Davos ski slope. As my *Observer* colleague William Keegan has shown, it has been around since at least 1869.

Today's Third Way has metamorphosed again, with its extremes now sharply drawn by global capital on one side and growing concerns for the environment on the other: Davos Man versus Seattle Man.

As a Third Way for business governments are everywhere decreasing their direct involvement in markets in favour of companies, increasingly using regulators and competition to hold the ring. In that sense, he predicted bluntly, companies in the future would run countries as much as governments did.

Third Way-ism also gets a boost, at least in the UK, from post-1997 developments in the labour market. The TUC's senior policy officer, David Coats, said that beneath the rhetoric of flexibility and deregulation, the Government has engineered a massive swing towards European mainstream social policy, signing up (with very little fuss) to the directives on working time, parental leave and part-time workers, as well as introducing the minimum wage, enacting statutory union recognition rights and greatly extending the rights of individuals at work.

But is 'stakeholding' enough? It's not just that the latest Workplace Employee Relations Survey shows just how small the inroads of such enlightenment have been at work. In other areas, companies seem part of the problem, not the solution.

Cranfield's Professor Joe Nellis repeatedly told the conference: 'Policy is a function of time and place.' The trouble is, the notions of time and place are themselves in a state of flux, so the best way of thinking about the Third Way may be not as 'in-betweenism' but as forever synthesising new ideas and rolling forward.

Some of the new ones, such as radical resource productivity, have barely been broached. Experiments with employee ownership need testing. Most firms don't know what to do about diversity, women, minorities, the young. And they are as crippled creatively as they are overdeveloped analytically.

Simon Caulkin, adapted from 'Third Way loses its bearings', *The Observer*, 6 February 2000

- The development of the '**New Deal**' for young people, the long-term unemployed and for older workers.
- An attempt to further deepen the enterprise society by encouraging wider share ownership, the removal of stigma from business failure and encouraging serial entrepreneurship.
- A broad consensus that the supply-side of industry should be encouraged against the macroeconomic background of fiscal and monetary stability.
- To undertake measures to improve the knowledge-based economy.
- Improvement in incentives to undertake R&D.
- Help to the small firm sector through the development of clustering and improvements in the venture capital industry.

- The introduction of the Working Time Directive and parental leave policies together with other 'family friendly' policies.
- Alterations in competition regulation and reforming the energy market and the regulation of utilities.
- In education, the main thrusts have been, in widening access into higher education, reducing class sizes for 5–7s and 7–9s, the naming and shaming of failing schools, and setting improvement targets for schools in terms of examination performances.
- Creating a climate for lifelong learning.
- Improving basic skills in literacy and numeracy.

Overall, the supply-side strategy of New Labour can be summed up in four words – stability, employability, productivity and responsibility.

Conclusions

The discussion of supply-side approaches to the economy used to be straightforward. Left wing governments became associated with Keynesian supply-side approaches, and from 1979 the Conservative governments were associated with new classical approaches. In the former approach, demand management was used to stabilise aggregate demand and because of market failure, Keynesians also prescribed policies such as indicative planning, nationalisation and various measures, both indirect (eg, fiscal carrots and sticks) and direct, to stimulate R&D and the investment in physical and human capital. There was certainly a complete change of attitude in the 1980s towards the way the UK economy should work. New classical economists believed in the freeing up of markets and the near complete reduction in government intervention in the market. In this respect through the 1980s and early 1990s we saw the freeing up of markets, the privatisation of state monopolies, rationalisation of the tax and social security system and the reform of trade unions amongst other policies.

The return of a Labour government to power in 1997 has not seen a return to the traditional Keynesian approaches to manage the economy. Instead what we have got has been called the 'Third Way'. A range of policies have been developed which are very much market based, relying on the market to provide incentives and for the free movement of capital; at the same time, the government's role is to provide stable economic provision and support for individuals. Also, the government has focused on the knowledge-based economy, entrepreneurship and innovation as a means to boost UK productivity. Although the government has stepped in with policies to improve the conditions facing labour (eg, the development of a raft of family friendly policies and the introduction of a minimum wage), and has altered competition policy, there is still great reliance on the market; however, there is an emphasis on encouraging individuals to take more responsibility for their own training and employability. It is to the detail of these policies that we now turn.

KEY WORDS

Keynesian view	Hayek
'Sticky' downwards	Austrian school
Discretionary fiscal and	Entrepreneurs
monetary policy	Third Way
Fine-tuning	Reskilling
Positive externalities	New Deal
Socially sub-optimal	Family friendly
New classical school	

Further reading

Beharrell, A. (1997), 'What are supply-side policies? How can they be used to reduce unemployment?', *Economics Today*, March, Vol. 4, No. 4, pp.9–12.

Congdon, T. (1996), 'Miracle vs. mirage: the Conservative economic record', *Economic Affairs*, Vol. 16, No. 4, pp.17–31.

Oliver, M. (1997), 'The Conservative years – a revolution in economic policy?', *Economic Review*, Vol. 15, No. 4, pp.23–27.

Romer, S. (1998), 'Has the government found a Third Way?', *Economics Today*, November, Vol. 6, No. 2, pp.10–12.

Vaughn, K.I. (2000), 'The re-birth of Austrian economics: 1974–99', Economic Affairs, Vol. 20, No.1, March, pp.40–43.

Useful websites

ECEDWEB: www.ecedweb.unomaha.edu/
Gateway site: www.open.gov.uk/
Central Office of Information: www.coi.gov.uk/

Essay topics

1. In 1991 the UK rate of inflation was 5.9 per cent and unemployment was 8.8 per cent. By June 1998 both inflation (2.8 per cent) and unemployment (4.8 per cent) had fallen significantly.
   (a) Examine the costs associated with (i) inflation and
       (ii) unemployment.   [50 marks]

(b) To what extent are policies designed to reduce the rate of inflation also appropriate for reducing unemployment? [50 marks]
[Edexcel, Paper 2, Q8, June 1999].

(a) Explain how fiscal and monetary policy can be used to influence the level of aggregate demand.　　　[20 marks]

(b) Should governments aim to influence aggregate demand, or should they concentrate on the supply-side of the economy?　　　[30 marks]
[AQA, Unit 6 Specimen Paper, Q3, 2000].

Chapter Four
Improving market efficiency

*'Privatisation is a key element of the Government's economic strategy
... Our main objective is to promote competition and increase
efficiency.'*
John Moore, Financial Secretary to the Treasury, 1983

Introduction

Public ownership has been in retreat in the UK since the early 1980s.
But switching organisations from the public to the private sector is not
always sufficient to improve the more efficient use of resources. Often
industries which are still believed to be natural monopolies in the private sector need to be regulated. At the same time that state-owned
industries have been switched to the private sector, the 1980s and
1990s saw a move to introduce market forces into the public sector
through the process of Compulsory Competitive Tendering (CCT). In
addition, as organisations were moved into the private sector, often
their markets were opened up to competitive forces through the
process of liberalisation or deregulation. As previously state-owned
assets came into the possession of the private sector this allowed other
organisations to purchase these. In an attempt to achieve the benefits
from more competition the government have needed to strengthen the
various pieces of competition regulation so that newly merged companies do not abuse their market position.

Privatisation in the UK

Privatisation was a central plank of the supply-side strategy pursued
by the post-1979 Conservative government. Ironically, however, the
Conservative government did not take power in 1979 with the idea of
privatising more than a handful of state-run companies. Initially, it
believed that public hostility to the idea of 'selling off the family silver'
and creating private monopolies out of nationalised industries would
limit the scope of privatisation to a small number of enterprises (eg,
the National Freight Corporation) for which there was little rationale
for public ownership. In the event, the early privatisations proved surprisingly popular, encouraging the Conservative governments of the
1980s to raise their sights until, eventually, giant corporations like
British Telecom, British Gas and the electricity and water industries
were sold off.

Table 6 lists the major privatisations to date. In total, the various UK governments sold over £70bn of state assets over the period 1979–98 (at 1998 prices), which have a current value in excess of £100bn.

Although privatisation of state assets was one approach to improving the supply-side of the economy, other methods were also used to draw upon private sector expertise such as the development of the **Private Finance Initiative** (PFI) in 1992. Under the PFI, government

Table 6 Major British privatisations

Mining, oil, agriculture and forestry
    British Coal, British Petroleum, Britoil, Enterprise Oil
    Land Settlement, Forestry Commission, Plant Breeding Institute
Electricity, gas and water
    British Gas
    National Power, Power Gen
    Nuclear Electric
    Northern Ireland Electric, Northern Ireland Generation
    Scottish Hydro Electric, Scottish Power
    National Grid
    Regional Electricity Distribution (12 companies)
    Regional Water Holding Companies (10 companies)
Manufacturing, science and engineering
    AEA Technology
    British Aerospace, Short Bros, Rolls-Royce
    British Shipbuilders, Harland and Wolff
    British Rail Engineering
    British Steel
    British Sugar Corporation
    Royal Ordnance
    Jaguar, Rover Group
    Amersham International
    British Technology Group Holdings (ICL, Fairey, Ferranti, Inmos)
Distribution, hotel and catering
    British Rail hotels
Transport and communications
    British Railways
    National freight, national and local bus companies
    Motorway service area leases
    Associated British Ports, trust ports, Sealink
    British Airways, British Airports Authority (and other airports)
    British Telecommunications, Cable and Wireless
Banking, finance, etc.
    Girobank

---

departments and agencies were transformed from owners and operators of assets to ongoing purchasers of services from the private sector. Private firms became long-term service providers not just asset builders. The main advantages of such schemes were that the government could draw upon private-sector management expertise and risk control. It also allowed the government to escape the initial cost of the project in exchange for future costs of 'renting' the building or the road. However, there are possible liabilities where costs increase outside the control of the private supplier.

With the election of the Blair government in 1997 we saw a change in the mood towards privatisation. Although privatisation had been attacked by the Labour Party whilst in opposition, opinions changed. Many privatisations appeared to be 'successful', there were few assets still in public ownership and returning private sector assets back to the state did not appear an electoral winner. The Labour Party therefore advocated a 'third way' – a form of **public-private partnership** (PPP). Here the private sector is brought into a service or organisation along with the public sector organisation but outright privatisation is avoided. Within the PPP, the PFI is seen as just a subdivision, albeit a large one, of a wide range of initiatives in which the public and private sectors are starting to work together in innovative ways. These would include hybrid privatisation: part-privatisation through PFI, part public sector, such as the London Underground; the 'wider markets initiative' where the public sector is starting to sell its skills, knowledge and assets to the private sector, operating as a salesperson rather than purchaser of services and the development of 'private sector companies with a public sector mission'.

Although PFI has now been subsumed under PPP, how has PFI worked? By December 1999 over 200 PFI deals had been signed which committed the government to £84bn in revenue expenditure over the next 25 years. In addition the government anticipates a further £11bn worth of capital value to be undertaken in the current three-year phase. The National Audit Office (NAO) has made an assessment of 11 of the 17 PFI deals. Although the reports are not a representative sample, few of them appear to come out as clear value for money. The best one, based upon how the deal was planned and how the bidding and contracting process was handled, was the social security department's privatisation of its offices. On the criteria used by the NAO, the Skye Bridge project appeared to be a rather 'fancy' way of borrowing money, and two of the four road deals were clearly more expensive than the public sector solution. Nonetheless, two other road contracts were judged as very good value for money. The prison service arrangements also had many positive aspects. The conclusion reached by the NAO is that each deal has to be judged on its own merits and that the government departments are improving in their use of PFI.

Privatisation and efficiency

While ideological and political factors have certainly influenced the privatisation programme since 1979, privatisation was primarily aimed at strengthening the performance of the supply-side of the economy. Ministers argued that, under public control, nationalised industries had no incentive to cut costs and respond to changing patterns of consumer demand. Since many nationalised industries enjoyed considerable monopoly power, they could easily achieve the crude financial objectives imposed on them by successive governments (eg, achieving a specified rate of return on capital investment) by manipulating their prices, rather than by cutting overstaffing and producing more efficiently.

Nationalised industries in the 1970s were characterised by considerable 'X-inefficiency' (ie, bureaucratic waste), overstaffing and ill-directed investment. Productivity growth in the nationalised sector lagged well behind that in the private sector and many enterprises made heavy financial losses which absorbed huge amounts of taxpayers' money. To the general public both at home and abroad, British nationalised industries were synonymous with over-priced, poor quality service.

However, given that most privatised industries continued to enjoy a significant degree of monopoly power after their transfer into the private sector, it is not immediately clear how precisely privatisation was intended to spur incumbent managements to greater efficiency. After all, the morning after privatisation, companies like British Telecom and British Gas – with the same managers and staff, and effectively unchallenged control of national, integrated distribution networks – faced no greater competition for customers than they had while in the public sector. For such companies, the new classical economist argued, the impetus to greater competition and efficiency lay in the new vulnerability of privatised enterprises to hostile takeover bids on the stock market.

Efficiency and profitability

The actual impact of privatisation on efficiency is, in fact, somewhat mixed. Efficiency might be measured in terms of industry profits. As organisations become more efficient they can increase their output per person and/or could see their cost base fall. Both would lead to

The golden era is over for water companies as the regulator starts to bite into profits. There are even whispers of renationalisation.

For 10 years the Ridleyite formula worked. Monopolist regional water and sewerage companies made fat profits but, under the loose supervision of a slide-rule-toting economist, were also required to invest heavily. Household bills were pushed up to make the balance sheets sing.

Water companies are being required to spend £15bn on investment during the next five years while cutting bills or at best keeping them constant. For the profit-oriented executives who succeeded the first post-privatisation generation of executives, watering England and Wales suddenly looks a lot less attractive. It is as if the PLCs are saying: if the state wants to regulate us hard, the state can have water back. Water privatisation could soon look like a mere episode, not the irreversible policy it was painted when Mrs Thatcher claimed (and was believed) to know where history was heading.

Last year the regulator, who retires this summer, got tough. Average household bills (up 40 per cent in real terms since privatisation) are to be held constant in cash terms till March 2005; they are being cut significantly this year. In April, Mr Byatt abstracted £700m or 12 per cent of the water PLCs' revenue. But he is still insisting on investments of nearly £3bn a year over the next half decade, for the sake of the environment, to ensure consistency of supply and to stem leaks.

Meanwhile the monopolists face another challenge – competition, or at least its threat. A water bill is in the offing which will carry forward the logic of the Competition Act 1998 and may force the water PLCs to open their pipes to other people's water, on the analogy of what has happened in gas and electricity. The water magnates respond that 'common carriage' could jeopardise safety and certainty of supply. Even though water companies themselves can now supply energy, even employ their networks for communications, the cosy arrangements of the past decade will have to give way. The political and corporate silence surrounding the latest price review suggests the PLCs have given up.

David Walker, adapted from, 'Don't tell Sid', *The Guardian*, 16 June 2000

increased profits. Yet on this basis BA's privatisation in the late 1990s could be measured as a failure. An increase in profits alone is not indicative of an improvement in efficiency. A monopoly producer is a price-setter and can choose to pitch prices at whatever level produces the desired level of profits. Nationalised industries, on the other hand, were under political control and were often instructed by the government of the day to charge lower, non-commercial prices on social grounds.

The problem of natural monopolies
Many of the enterprises that have been privatised are **natural monopo-**

lies, in which the creation of effective competition is highly problematic. Moreover, in the case of natural monopolies like electricity, gas and water, not only does the transfer of ownership risk consumer exploitation, but it may also result in the industries becoming less, rather than more, efficient in terms of average production costs. This is because natural monopolies arise in industries that are characterised by declining average cost functions; that is, as output increases, costs continuously decline, so that as soon as one firm grows slightly larger than its rivals, it enjoys a self-reinforcing cost-advantage which allows it to grow and cut costs until it has captured the whole market.

Given that, by definition, it is counter-productive to break-up a natural monopoly, the task facing the government was to find a means of transferring such enterprises into the private sector, while at the same time encouraging new management to hold down costs and prices. In Britain, as in many other countries, the solution has been to design a system of **regulation** which, to a large extent, replaces the hidden political control over pricing and output decisions that existed in the past.

The role of regulation

The privatised monopolies are regulated by terms laid down in their privatisation legislation and their operating licences. For example, British Telecom, which was the first major utility to be privatised, has an operating license which runs for 25 years in the first instance. This sets out the terms under which the utility must operate, including the supply of rural services, telephone boxes and emergency calls. Prices are largely regulated by a predetermined formula and the regulatory system is policed by the Office of Telecommunications (OFTEL). This structure has been copied for gas, water and electricity.

The method of price control that has been introduced in Britain was designed to overcome the main disadvantages of US-style regulation. The 'retail price index (RPI) minus X' formula, as it is known, was intended to control prices while permitting increased profits resulting from lower costs. The regulators would fix the X factor on the basis of forecast productivity gains in comparable industries (eg, 2 per cent per annum). If the privatised industry achieved productivity growth in line with this sectoral average, it could then raise its prices each year by 2 per cent less than the inflation rate, maintaining a broadly constant rate of return. Productivity improvements in excess of 2 per cent would accordingly enable it to increase its rate of return for the same permitted price rise. Furthermore, the UK system of control is a discretionary one where the regulator, who has detailed knowledge of the

Table 7 Telecoms and the regulatory formula

Formula	Time period
RPI – 3	1984–89
RPI – 4.5	1989–91
RPI – 6.25	1991–93
RPI – 7.5	1993–97
RPI – 4.5	1997–2000

industry, can be argued to be in a position of greater understanding than the government or the Office of Fair Trading.

However, despite the advantages of the RPI minus X formula over direct rate of return controls, it does contain a major flaw which can lead to inefficiencies. In practice, it appears that the X factor is periodically reassessed, in the light of what the regulatory body considers to be a 'satisfactory' rate of profit. Table 7 shows the way that the formula has been used in telecoms to reflect the changing profits of BT.

It is important to note that, with regard to the telecoms market, not all of this is controlled by the regulator. The unregulated parts include: payphone calls, customer premises equipment, telex, mobile radio, leased lines, etc. In addition, if the 'X' is set too low, because the regulator has underestimated the ability of the organisation to make cost cuts, then large profits can occur. For example, excessive profits in the water industry led to OFWAT ordering the water companies to make an average 10 per cent price cut in 2000. Such an approach leads to the removal of any incentive for the organisation to cut costs. Further, the regulator becomes very important in the performance of the industries and it is impossible to tell whether their objectives are the same as the government. Because regulators develop a close relationship between themselves and senior managers of the organisations they are trying to control, some of them may increasingly see the issues from the organisation's point of view – the so-called '**regulatory capture**'. Regulation is also not free. There are costs in running the regulatory offices and costs for the regulated company which need to supply information to the regulator. In addition, further costs may be incurred by the organisation as it tries to anticipate the changes that the regulator might make.

The performance of privatised companies
The locus of improved economic performance after privatisation has

often focused on productive efficiency gains producing a given amount at minimum cost. That is, not only producing at a point of technical efficiency but also price efficiency. In terms of performance it is important to distinguish between short-run effects and long-run effects, with the latter dealing with **dynamic efficiency gains**, the development of new products and the discovery of new methods of working. If we consider what happened generally to the privatised industries in terms of profits, prices, output and productivity, initial research during the 1980s suggested that performance had generally improved in all these areas, but that the performance gains tended to precede actual privatisation. This might beg the question why privatisation was needed at all, but it could indicate that the improved performance would not have taken place if privatisation had not been on the horizon.

The broad consensus seems to be that in cases where the costs of market failure arising from monopoly power are insignificant, transfer of ownership to the private sector will produce technical efficiency gains by providing the incentives to minimise costs. Where market failure occurs because monopoly power is significant, then there is the need for a regulatory framework. However, where the regulatory framework is imperfect and when the costs of regulation are taken into account then the link between privatisation of state-owned monopolies and economic performance is unclear. In fact it might be possible to get the technical efficiency gains by restructuring the public enterprise.

There is no unique measure of **technical efficiency**. Moreover since accounting records do not usually contain sufficient information about costs, empirical analysis has to use other indicators such as productivity measures to infer changes in efficiency. Even then it is difficult to extract these changes from changes that occur to an organisation through the process of the business cycle. For privatised companies which faced some degree of competition, a comparison in 1995 of the post-privatisation period and the period just before privatisation with the period during which the organisation was in state ownership, labour productivity gains were to be found in British Airways, Britoil, British Aerospace, British Gas, British Telecom and National Freight. If capital changes are also taken into account then only British Airways emerges with gains as compared to the nationalisation period, and in fact the most significant gains are to be found in the period just prior to privatisation.

In the context of employment privatisation has resulted in over 750,000 jobs being transferred to private ownership between 1984 and 1999, but in many of the privatised sectors, employment has fallen substantially such as in British Gas, Corus (British Steel), the rail companies and British Telecom. Some have seen employment rising such as the British Airports Authority whilst in others employment has fluctuated more widely, being more heavily dependent on winning outside contracts and through the process of merger/acquisition and demergers.

Profitability has varied markedly too. British Telecom, the electricity-generating companies and the electricity distributors and water companies have made fairly large profits year-on-year. However, some companies such as BA have posted losses during the latter part of the 1990s, having achieved large profits during the early 1990s.

Customers have benefited from improved services and prices. A 1996 study from the NAO found that service had improved significantly in telecoms and to a lesser extent in electricity, gas and water since privatisation. Most customers are also paying less for their utility bills. Since privatisation, the average telephone bill has declined in real terms by 49 per cent. In the gas industry where it has taken longer to introduce competition, the average domestic gas bill has fallen by 31 per cent since privatisation and the average electricity bill by 20 per cent. Conversely, the average water and sewerage bills have increased by 36 per cent and 42 per cent, respectively, due to the argument that British water companies have had to invest large sums of money to meet European environmental standards. There is, however, a valid argument that many of these post-privatisation improvements and price cuts owed as much to changes in technology and the decline in fossil-fuel prices as they did to changes in ownership. In addition there is some resentment that a number of the original privatised sales were under-priced and that a number of the managers had received 'fat-cat' salaries.

What does emerge from a range of studies on privatised companies is that the regulatory regime of the price cap mechanism has faced regulators with a sharp learning curve. Furthermore, depending on the sector, the manner in which privatisation was carried out allowed some organisations to retain their vertically integrated structures, therefore preventing the full benefits of competition from being reaped.

Although the privatisation of public utilities by the various Conservative administrations during the 1980s and early 1990s received the greatest headlines, the various Conservative administrations also tried to get different departments or components within a particular part of the public sector to trade with one another as a means of encouraging competition and efficiency. Examples of this can be found in education with the development of devolved budgets where, through the locally managed schools scheme (LMS), schools have to all intents and purposes become self-financing. Perhaps one of the most comprehensive and controversial attempts at introducing market relationships could be found in the health service through the development of hospital trusts, GP budget holders and the like.

Contracting out

Not only were large nationalised industries viewed with suspicion, but Conservative perceptions during 1979–97 were that local authorities were inefficient, wasted public money, were unaccountable and a threat to political stability. Labour councils could undermine Conservative government budgetary control and in order to reduce this countervailing power, local authorities were subject to rate-capping, a change to the poll tax and the introduction of contracting out or competitive tendering.

Compulsory competitive tendering (CCT) was introduced under the 1980 Local Government Planning and Land Act and covered services such as highways, buildings and maintenance work. This process was further extended in 1988 under the Local Government Act which extended CCT to refuse collection, cleaning, catering, ground mainte-nance and vehicle maintenance and further amended through 'Best Value' in January 2000. The government argued that market testing through the process of contracting out held many advantages:

- competition should ensure value for money;
- by focusing on performance, outputs would produce clear stan-dards;
- the quality of services would be improved;
- an explicit customer/supplier relationship would be apparent;
- both internal and external bidders could be more innovative in their proposals;
- by focusing on outputs, objectives and targets, there would be improvements in efficiency and effectiveness.

The results of the process of contracting out have been mixed. Almost three-quarters of contracts put out to tender have been won in-house. There have been variations by service with around 70 per cent of refuse and street collection contracts, over 95 per cent of catering con-tracts and around 55 per cent of building cleaning contracts remaining in-house.

As to the efficiency gains, studies appeared to show conflicting reports. All noted that costs tended to be lower after the contract had been won through the competitive tendering process, but as to whether contracting out gave the greater cost reduction as compared with the contract remaining in-house, the surveys remain inconclusive. Nonetheless, the surveys did suggest that cost reductions were more likely to arise through reductions in wages and longer hours rather than efficiency gains. There are also issues of public accountability to consider as the private sector organisation is responsible for the service not the local authority or government department.

Deregulation

Some privatisations have been accompanied by **deregulation** and it is often argued that it is the latter, rather than the former, that actually promotes competition. For instance, the privatisation of British Telecom (BT) in 1985 was preceded by the 1981 Telecommunications Act, which permitted certain kinds of private equipment to be connected to the BT network and allowed a newly-formed private consortium, Mercury (now part of Cable and Wireless), to compete for domestic business. As a result of the 1981 Act, new products, such as car telephones and more sophisticated receivers, have mushroomed.

The objectives of deregulation are to increase competition between existing suppliers and between them and new suppliers who can now enter the market. This should reduce costs and stimulate the provision of new services for which there is a demand.

The real issue here is one of the 'grid'. Generally many privatised industries are not natural monopolies but it is the grid which is the monopoly. In the case of the gas and water industries it is the pipelines, for electricity it is the power lines, etc. Thus one way to improve competition is to make access easier to these local or national grids. An alternative approach has also been adopted in the separation of ownership of the 'grid' from supplying companies. Hence British Gas was separated into pipeline and supplying companies and the national electricity grid was re-privatised in 1996, separating out the grid part from the 12 regional electricity companies.

Since 1998, there has been free competition in supplying gas to any homes or businesses – though there is some criticisms of the hard sell made by sales representatives of the various companies and that the low rate of supplier switching has been due to the contractual differences which make prices hard to compare. The electricity sector has also been opened up to free competition since 1999.

It is not just in the supply to customers that competition has grown. There has also been an increase in the number of gas producers and electricity generators. The telecommunications market, too, has become more competitive with the growth of mobile phones and lines supplied by cable operators. The incumbent privatised companies have also been prevented from using their dominant position as a barrier to entry to new firms. For example, British Gas, since 1995, has had to limit its share of the industrial gas market to 40 per cent.

Although deregulation has led to more **contestable markets,** the privatised companies are still huge and there is scope for other forms of collusive behaviour. Therefore, whilst the price cap system has been progressively abandoned as competition has increased, the regulators have had to operate more like the Office of Fair Trading (OFT) to prevent collusion and the abuse of monopoly power. The regulators have the right to intervene through the relevant Acts of Privatisation and through the 1998 Competition Act.

Competition policy

At a UK, European and global level there has been a tendency for large firms to develop through market forces as size is seen as a pre-requisite for long-term existence in the global market place. As an example of this we need look no further than the changes that have taken place in the media sector through the development of large global media corporations such as Time Warner and in the car industry, where excess global capacity has been reduced through merger and take over, eg Ford's merger with Fiat in 2000. Allowing such firms to develop may give them distinct advantages but at the same time it provides the opportunity for markets to behave inefficiently. Thus there are supply-side problems.

But what type of **competition policy** might be developed? There are no hard and fast rules, but there may be some useful starting points. Differences in market structure may affect the competitive behaviour of firms. Markets that are highly competitive are unlikely to lead to organisations whose performance could reduce market welfare. On the other hand, it is not always possible to say that markets which are oligopolistic or where there is a single provider will lead to reductions in economic welfare. Oligopolists, for example, can behave both competitively and cooperatively. In the case of uncompetitive behaviour by organisations, it may be possible to consider an organisation's performance against some industry norm, or against a similar sized organisation. However, it must be recognised that organisations which make high level of profits may be doing so because they are very efficient at controlling costs rather than charging high prices. In addition it is important to consider what happens to these profits over time. Are they short term or have they been in existence over longer periods? Are current levels of profits acceptable as a return for previous R&D and will profits be eroded in the future as new firms seek to enter the market?

Consideration should also be given to contestability of markets. Evidence which shows the movement of firms into and out of an industry may suggest that the market is contestable and that economic welfare is not being harmed. Conversely, where markets do not appear to be contestable then entry barriers may be being used and competition policy needs to consider how these barriers can be reduced.

Competition policy, therefore, should be designed to promote more competition or to prevent a reduction in competition. The problem for economists is that they find it difficult to agree on the conditions necessary to best promote competition. It follows therefore, that the type of competition policy advocated differs. If we are concerned about market structure and the ramifications that flow from this then competition policy should attempt to change market structure and impose constraints on the behaviour of firms. That is, barriers to entry should be reduced, monopolies should be broken up or regulated and there should be attempts to stop organisations reaching a dominant position through a mergers policy. Competition policy should actively prevent organisations from abusing their dominant market positions via resale price maintenance and by using restrictive practices.

Conversely, the Austrian view is that competition policy is required to ease entry into markets. These barriers to entry may be erected by the private sector but from the Austrian school perspective are likely to be government-imposed barriers. The Austrian approach is to reject market intervention because this distorts the market process. Further, the Austrian school would argue that no single organisation has the power to distort the competition within a market anyway. If monopoly power exists, it is because that is the most efficient system for the market.

UK competition policy

Although we wish to concentrate on changes in competition policy since 1979, the various acts that were produced to encourage competition in the market were developments or modifications of earlier acts.

- The Monopolies and Restrictive Practices Act (1948) established the MMC and defined a monopoly as a firm or group of firms which act together to control one-third or more of a market.
- The 1965 Monopolies and Mergers Act provided for the investigation of mergers and acquisitions which might produce or strengthen a monopoly, if they involved a takeover of assets in excess of £5 million.
- The 1973 Fair Trading Act altered the definition of a unitary monopoly to one where a single firm controlled 25 per cent or more

of the market and where these sales can be defined at a national, regional or local level. Mergers could also be investigated where they involve 25 per cent or more market shares or where at least £30 million worth of assets were taken over.

- The Competition Act of 1980, although concerned with anti-competitive practices, also extended monopoly control and provision to the nationalised industries and other public sector bodies.
- The Companies Act of 1989 modified merger legislation in three ways. First, the companies involved must provide a formal pre-notification of their activity. Second, even if the Director of Fair Trading had recommended that the Secretary of State should refer the merger to the MMC, if the firms agreed to sell off some of their assets to decrease their excess power, then the merger may still be allowed to take place. Third, once the merger has been referred to the MMC, the companies are prohibited from acquiring each other's shares.
- Finally, the Competition Act of 1998, which came into force in March 2000, has brought UK competition more in line with that in the EU. The 1998 Act deals with both vertical and horizontal price fixing, agreements to share out markets, agreements to limit production, agreements to coordinate or limit investment, collusive tendering, and problems with the sharing of information and the boycotting of suppliers and firms that deal with competitors. It also made existing policies towards firms with a dominant position much tougher, and replaced the MMC with the Competition Commission.

EU competition policy

In addition to national legislation, organisations within the EU and UK are increasingly subject to EU policies in these areas. The EU has no power where the effects of a monopoly or takeover are confined to one member state, but on the occasions of contention between national and EU law, the latter takes precedence.

The main provisions of EU competition policy are Articles 81 and 82 of the Treaty of Rome (these used to be Articles 85 and 86, but the numbering was altered after the Amsterdam Treaty in 1997).

- Article 81 prohibits restrictive agreements between companies affecting or leading to distortion of competition within the Community.
- Article 82 prohibits the use of a dominant position within the Community by organisations.

Conclusions

Privatisation in its many guises has been a central plank of supply-side policy over the last two decades, although the results have been mixed. The attempt to pursue three broad goals, namely, increasing efficiency, widening share ownership and reducing the PSBR, have led to inevitable conflicts in policy. The theoretical case for privatisation relies upon a particularly pessimistic view of motivation in the public sector, alongside an optimistic view of the disciplining effect on management of exposure to the commercial capital market.

Economic theory and the international evidence suggest that competition, rather than ownership, is the key to ensuring high operating efficiency. The existence of privatised natural monopolies, which face no significant competition, has necessitated a regulatory structure for each industry. In effect, privatisation has simply altered the form of regulation – from political direction to arm's length control by the means of regulatory bodies. Given the pivotal role of these natural monopolies in the economy, it is difficult to see how any government could abdicate responsibility for their behaviour. Moreover, even if privatisation has removed the inefficiencies resulting from direct political intervention, it has introduced new distortions, notably in terms of price control, and opened up the risk of regulatory capture and regulatory muddle.

After years of criticism of Conservative privatisation policies, the new Labour government has not sought to turn back towards national ownership but through its policy of PPP has hoped to foster closer links between the private and public sector. At the same time Competition Policy has been extended and developed to match more closely that which exists within the EU. It remains to be seen whether this 'third-way' will improve the performance of the privatised sectors of the economy.

KEY WORDS

Privatisation	Dynamic efficiency gains
Private Finance Initiative	Technical efficiency
Public-private partnership	Compulsory competitive
X-inefficiency	tendering
Natural monopolies	Deregulation
Regulation	Contestable markets
Regulatory capture	Competition policy

Further reading

Bamford, C. (1998), Chapter 5 in, *Transport Economics*, 2nd edn, Studies in Economics and Business, Heinemann Educational.

Hurl, B. (1995), *Privatization and the Public Sector*, 3rd edn, Heinemann Educational.

Maunder, P. (1998), 'Competition policy in the UK and the EU', in *Developments in Economics: Annual Review*, ed. G.B.J. Atkinson, Vol. 14, Causeway Press, pp. 117–131.

Munday, S. (2000), Chapter 5 in, *Markets and Market Failure*, Studies in Economics and Business, Heinemann Educational.

Smith, D. (2000), Chapter 3 in, *UK Current Economic Policy*, 2nd edn, Studies in Economics and Business, Heinemann Educational.

Useful websites

House of Commons: http://www.parliament.uk/commons/selcom89

Monopolies and Mergers Commission: http://www.mmc.gov.UK/speeches.htm

Economist: http://www.economist.com/

Essay topics

1. 'Once a market such as the telecommunications market or the water market becomes sufficiently contestable, regulation is no longer needed.'
   (a) Choosing a utility industry, such as the telecommunications or water industry, explain the factors which affect the contestability of the market. [20 marks]
   (b) Assess the case for and against abolishing the agency, such as OFTEL and OFWAT , which is currently responsible for regulating the industry. [30 marks]
   [AQA, Unit 5 Specimen Paper, Q2, 2000].
2. (a) Explain the link between government competition policy and aggregate supply. [10 marks]
   (b) Assess the case for and against privatising the UK's air traffic control industry. [10 marks]

Data response question

This task is based on a question set by Edexcel in 1999.

Since Labour's victory in last year's election, the Tory record of privatisation has been treated by ministers as a regrettable, albeit irreversible, act of short-sighted greed. John Prescott, the Deputy Prime Minister, who is in overall charge of transport policy, has singled out the way British Rail was privatised, accusing the rolling-stock companies of 'having grown fat at the tax-payer's expense'.

This view has left Labour with a problem about what to do with remaining state assets that might benefit from private sector methods and investment. For example, in opposition, Labour attacked plans to privatise air traffic control as 'crazy'. In government, it now sees the advantages of using private money for the expensive capital investment needed by the service. Typically, the solution now is to search for a 'third way' — some form of public-private partnership, in which private money is brought into the service but outright privatisation is avoided.

Labour's reluctance to use the privatisation word is oddly out of tune with its usual tendency to trumpet any successful British export. For privatisation is one British invention that continues to be emulated around the world. Flotations of privatised assets are expected to take place in more than 100 countries in 1995–2000 and to raise over £120 billion ($200 billion). The reasons for this are not hard to understand: privatisation works, as any fair reading of the British record amply illustrates.

First, the benefits to British public finances over the past two decades have been considerable. The cumulative proceeds from privatisation between 1979 and 1997 were more than £90 billion (at current prices). Customers have also benefited. A 1996 study from the National Audit Office found that service had improved significantly in telecoms and, to a lesser extent, in electricity, gas and water since privatisation. Most customers are also paying

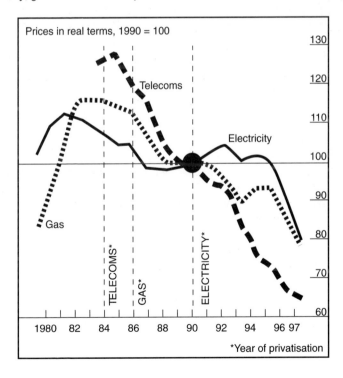

less for their utility bills. But even in industries where it has taken time to introduce competition, regulation has meant that prices have fallen as the figure above shows. Water and sewerage are the exceptions: average domestic household bills rose by 36 per cent and 42 per cent respectively. Water apart, the dramatic improvements in price and service give the lie to the claim that customers have been the prime victims of privatisation. Another frequently voiced fear was that privatisation would lead to a deterioration in safety. The evidence points the other way.

Yet facts alone do not seem enough to win the argument. Market research suggests that privatisation has never been wildly popular, and that it has been getting less so as time goes by. In 1983, 43 per cent of people wanted more privatisation; by 1992 that was down to 24 per cent, and in 1997 a poll found just 19 per cent in favour of privatising the Underground.

Why is this? Many people believe that the most recent privatisations do not make sense, because it is hard to introduce competition in some industries, such as rail. But this ignores the role of regulation in mimicking competition — something that has improved the electricity and gas industries, even though the introduction of real competition is only now being completed. Furthermore, the privatised industries, particularly gas and water, played into their critics' hands with their inept management of boardroom pay.

Public awareness of the fact that the new owners of nationalised industries did well for themselves may have increased the tendency to complain about examples of poor service. The regulators have certainly noticed a sharp increase in complaints about privatised services, rail and water in particular. Some regulators have themselves been critical of the performance of privatised undertakings; for example OFWAT has criticised water companies for the slow progress in reducing leakages in pipes. But most of these complaints and mistakes are the teething pains of a huge structural economic change.

Source: *The Economist,* 13 June 1998.

(a) In terms of economic efficiency, outline the economic case for governments selling state-owned undertakings.   [10 marks]

(b) Discuss the impact of privatisation in the UK on consumers, taxpayers, shareholders and those employed in former state-owned undertakings.   [20 marks]

(c) Evaluate the effectiveness of the systems created to regulate the privatised utilities.   [20 marks]

Chapter Five

Strengthening the labour market

'The issue of flexibility of the labour market is central to the current debate on: competitiveness; globalisation; the reduction of unemployment; job creation; and the viability and legitimacy of the European social model.'
Hedva Sarfati, 1999

Introduction

An important dimension of government supply-side policies over the last twenty years has been the reform of the labour market. This has been tackled in a number of ways. The tax and social security system has been overhauled to encourage individuals back into the labour market, providing support for working mothers and the like. In addition there have been a raft of policies aimed at reforming trade unions. At the same time flexibility and mobility within the labour market have been promoted and policies have been used to improve the education and training of the workforce. Although the introduction of minimum wages within the UK could be seen as reducing labour market flexibility, in the short term it has not had the detrimental effect expected on labour supply and has even encouraged some people to participate in the labour market. It is to the whole area of supply-side policies that have been used to strengthen the labour market that this chapter now turns.

The New Deal

Amongst the new initiatives aimed at improving and building upon previous labour market reform, the Labour government has emphasised getting young workers and the long-term unemployed back into work. The '**New Deal**', introduced in 1998, attempts to close the gap between the skills employers want and the skills people can offer. There are a number of specific groups at which the New Deal is aimed. First, it has been targeted at the 18–24 year age group who have been claiming Jobseekers Allowance for six months for more. A second group at which the New Deal is aimed is lone parents who have been looking after at least one school-aged child on their own, and claiming income support. Third, there is the New Deal for people aged 25 or over and who have been unemployed for two years or more. The participants in the New Deal scheme have a number of options. They may go into full-time education and training, the Environment Task Force or the voluntary sector.

The New Deal as a whole is a partnership scheme between employers, local authorities, training providers, Learning and Skills Council, Local Enterprise Companies, Job Centres, environment groups, voluntary organisations and others. It is also said to have the advantage that the service is tailored to the needs of individuals, supporting them while they prepare for work and find a job, and delivering skills and training that are relevant to local jobs. For those who do not participate in the scheme, sanctions are supposed to be levied which reduce their level of benefits.

The New Deal, however, is not without its critics. First, there has been a fairly high drop-out rate from the scheme. Second, even for those who have completed the scheme, the take-up into full-time employment has not as been as high as expected; and third, there have been fewer cases than expected against which the sanctions have been levelled. On a more positive note, by November 1999, in the first two years of the New Deal for younger people, the programme had dealt with 329,000 clients and of these, 133,000 entered sustained jobs (lasting more than 13 weeks). Evaluation, however, of the whole scheme is difficult since the scheme is aimed at different age groups

Table 8 Training schemes to help the unemployed

Year	16–18 year olds	18–24 year olds
1978	Youth Opportunity Programme (YOP)	
1983	Youth Training Scheme (YTS)	
1986	2 year YTS	
1990	Youth Training (YT) to replace YTS	Employment Training (ET), Employment Action
1993		Training for Work Learning for Work Community Action
1994		Accelerated Modern Apprenticeships
1995	Modern Apprenticeships Youth Credits Continuation of YT	Workwise
1998	New Deal	New Deal

and within these age groups are clients who have different needs and expectations.

The New Deal follows on from a range of provisions that have been introduced since 1978 to improve the skills of individuals and help them back into the job market (Table 8).

Tax and social security reform

Other areas of the tax and benefit system have also been reformed with the introduction of the **minimum wage** (see later in this chapter), the reform of **National Insurance** contributions, the introduction of **working-tax credit** and a **child-care tax credit** together with the introduction of a 10 per cent starting rate of income tax.

Over the last twenty years there has also been a move in the UK economy away from direct taxation towards indirect taxation. Nonetheless, the tax burden, expressed as the total tax take to National Income, has on the whole returned to levels seen during the early part of the 1980s, even with the rhetoric of both parties trying to explain that they are tax-cutting parties. However, in relative terms the UK is only a middle-ranking country with regard to its tax burden, lying below many Scandinavian countries and both France and Germany. There also does not appear to be any strong correlation between tax burden and economic growth. Finland which had the third highest tax burden between 1981 and 1997 had a growth rate on average of 2.3 per cent during this period, whereas, Switzerland, which had one of the lowest tax burdens had a growth rate of 1.2 per cent during the same period.

Local taxes have also been changed quite dramatically over the last twenty years. The short-lived Community Charge in England and Wales was introduced during 1990, along with the **Uniform Business Rate** in the same year. However, the unpopularity of the 'poll tax' led to it being replaced in 1993 by the Council Tax.

In addition to the changes that have taken place to streamline the taxation system and to use tax changes as an incentive towards higher productivity, there have also been changes in the social security system. One major modification occurred in 1988 that affected unemployment benefits, pensions, income support, housing benefits, a family credit system and the social funds. The **State Earnings Related Pensions Scheme** (SERPS) which provided a pension based upon National Insurance contributions was reduced. Individuals could, if they wished, contract out of SERPS. Similarly, the supplementary benefit and heating allowances were abolished and a new system of income support was introduced.

Policies to encourage labour force participation

As a means to encourage more active job search by those unemployed, the Labour administration further developed the **Jobseeker's Allowance** introduced in 1996. The Jobseeker's Allowance involved a form of contractual arrangement between an Employment Service Adviser and the unemployed person specifying what was to be undertaken by both parties as a means of encouraging individuals back into work. In April 1998 the Labour administration took this procedure further forward through the New Deal or '**Welfare to Work**' initiative as outlined earlier in this chapter.

As a further move to encourage the move from welfare into work a single organisation, the Contributions Agency, was set up for the self-employed and small businesses to reduce the amount of red tape. In addition, in April 1999 over 1 million people were made exempt of employers' National Insurance contributions as the limit was raised, thereby decreasing the cost of employing these workers.

The new Labour administration have also sought to introduce a range of family friendly policies as a means of encouraging mothers, in particular, back into the workforce. There have been a number of both voluntary measures and statutory rights introduced to push forward family friendly policies both at the large and the small and medium sized enterprise level. These include:

- a national child-care strategy to meet the needs of children and support their parents in combining work and family life
- the development of ways to encourage working from home by raising its status
- the development of Working Tax Credit, giving financial support to working families
- the **Working Time Directive,** enabling people to balance better their work and home lives
- the Parental Leave Directive, giving both parents the right to three months unpaid leave after the birth or adoption of a child
- the extension of maternity leave arrangements.

In addition, the current Labour government is also seeking to provide time off from work for families when there are emergencies, and have guaranteed part-time workers the same rights (pro rata) as full-time workers.

Trades unions and economic growth

In addition to distorting the smooth functioning of the supply-side in an asymmetric way, the Conservative administrations also accused trades unions of inhibiting private sector R&D and investment in physical and human capital. The trade union movement in Britain has historically been 'craft-based', with workers joining unions that cover their particular occupation (eg, printing or engineering). The monopoly power of an individual trade union thus resides in its power to control labour of a specific functional type. For example, a nationally-based engineering union can bargain with employers from a very powerful base, since companies will find it very difficult to recruit qualified engineering workers who are not union members.

One potential disadvantage of this union structure in Britain is that it may militate against supply-side change. R&D and investment strengthen the economy by improving productivity; that is, by changing the way that people work in ways that increases output per head. The argument is, therefore, that since economic growth necessarily involves continuously redefining workers' jobs and functional responsibilities, old craft-based trades unions which have a duty to protect the jobs of their membership from structural change inhibit R&D and investment in new products and processes. Trades unions retort that, provided employers are prepared to retrain and upgrade the skills of their existing workforce, rather than discard them in favour of better qualified outsiders whenever job specifications change, there need be no conflict between job security and structural change. Whatever the rights and wrongs of this ongoing debate, it is the government's concern that unions may not only inhibit the flexibility of the labour market but also retard economic change.

Trade union legislation

Since 1979, a series of statutes has placed restrictions on trade union activity. The government has targeted two aspects of trades unions in particular: first, their ability to undertake strike action, and second, their right to enforce a '**closed shop**' (an arrangement whereby all employees within a company must belong to a recognised trade union).

- The 1980 Employment Act made secondary picketing illegal.
- The 1982 Employment Act specified that a lawful trade dispute must 'wholly or mainly' relate to employment matters, in an attempt to prevent political strikes.
- The 1984 Trade Union Act required industrial action to be formally approved in advance by the union members concerned in a secret ballot.
- The 1988 Employment Act gave union members the right not to be disciplined by their union for failing to take part in industrial

action, further weakening a union's ability to mobilize an effective strike.

- The 1990 Employment Act made it unlawful to deny people a job on the grounds that they are not union members.
- The 1992 Trade Union and Labour Relations (Consolidation Act) specified details of union ballots and the regulation of unions' financial affairs. It further stated the conditions for a union to expel or discipline a member and made it unlawful for employers to penalise workers for joining or refusing to join a union.
- The Trade Union Reform and Employment Rights Act (1993), extended the provisions of the 1992 Act effectively ending the closed shop, required employers to obtain workers' written permission before union due could be deducted from their pay packets and required all union ballots to be postal. The requirement that trade union members had to give their written consent to have union subscriptions deducted from their pay was repealed in 1998 as it was seen as threatening union membership levels.
- The Employment Relations Act of 1999, which came into operation in September 2000, further modified earlier changes in industrial relations covering areas such as collective bargaining where trade unions must be recognised in organisations where there are 21 employees or more (if that is the wish of the majority of the workforce), ballots, unfair dismissal, training where employers must meet workers to discuss training policy and practice, part-time work where workers are given the same rights pro rata as full-time workers, and leave for family and domestic reasons.

Impact of legislation on trade unions

The results of this legislative onslaught on the trade union movement have been profound. Although it is difficult to disentangle the effects of the new laws (which have tended to reduce the benefits of union membership) from those resulting from structural economic change (which have altered the composition of the employed labour force, creating female, part-time jobs at the expense of traditional, full-time manual employment), the fact remains that between 1979 and 2000, union density[1] fell (see Figure 9).

Nonetheless, actual trade union membership has begun to grow during the first part of the new millennium due mainly to the increase in the numbers of individuals in employment. It has also been interesting to note that the Labour administration since 1997 has not repealed many of the earlier Acts of the past 18 years but has modified them when and where they see necessary. It may be expected

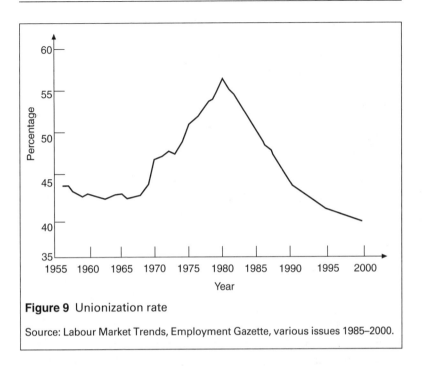

Figure 9 Unionization rate

Source: Labour Market Trends, Employment Gazette, various issues 1985–2000.

that trade union density will further rise in the future given the changes in trade union recognition involved in the Employment Relations Act of 1999.

A further indicator of the success of the various governments' new legal framework for wage bargaining has been the marked fall in the number of days lost through industrial disputes (see Figure 10). Although there was a sudden surge in days lost during the protracted and highly divisive miners' strike of 1984–85, the underlying trend since 1979 appears to have been firmly downwards with the UK having the eighth lowest number of working days lost through strikes in 1998 per thousand employees in the OECD.

At the same time that Conservative administrations were seeking to curb the power of trade unions, the UK's membership of the EU threw up equally significant, and some would say opposing, legislation within the labour market framework. The European **Social Charter,** is a statement of intent that by itself does not create legally enforceable rights. Nonetheless it has put forward rights in the areas of individual freedom of movement of workers, the right of training, health and safety protection, minimum rules on work duration amongst others. In particular it included rights for employees in the participation of deci-

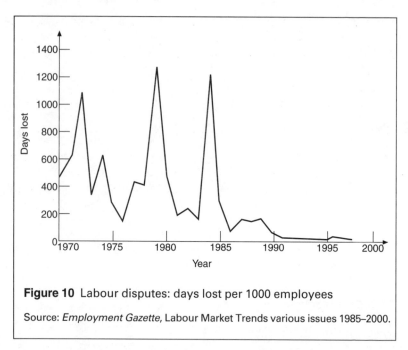

Figure 10 Labour disputes: days lost per 1000 employees

Source: *Employment Gazette*, Labour Market Trends various issues 1985–2000.

sions on redundancies and closures and in the setting up of workers' councils.

The Conservative administration of the early 1990s obtained an opt out from the Social Chapter provisions of the Social Charter, but this opt out was reversed in 1997. This meant that the UK was now able to adopt a range of directives that were already in operation in other member states. These directives included the Working Time Directive which specified an upper working time limit for a number of occupations, the Parental Leave Directive giving parents the right to three months unpaid parental leave after the birth of a child, and the Part-time Workers' Directive which gave part-time workers the same rights as full-time workers.

Promoting flexibility and mobility in the labour market

The governments of the past two decades have also had the objective of 'improving the **flexibility of the labour market**'. Flexibility can take on many guises, but in broad terms relates to people more suitable for, and adaptable to, employment needs, which are themselves changing rapidly. In this respects it includes:

- Wage or earnings flexibility – the responsiveness of wages to market pressure. At the micro level it is about matching pay with productivity. At the macro level this is the degree to which payment responds to changes in the demand and supply of labour.

- **Labour mobility** – the ability of individuals to move between regions, occupations and jobs and including the level of movement within a company.
- **Functional flexibility** – reducing the demarcation lines between different occupations.
- Flexibility in the pattern and organisation of work.

The impetus for these policies was inspired by the apparent increase in the **natural rate of unemployment** during the 1970s and 1980s. It follows that the more difficult it is for people to move smoothly between jobs – either because their skills do not match up precisely with the jobs on offer or because they live in a different part of the country from the location of the new jobs – the longer workers are temporarily unemployed while switching jobs. The government has accordingly laid great emphasis on the need to promote occupational and geographical labour mobility, in an effort to bring down the natural rate of unemployment.

Occupational mobility

Although there are sound supply-side reasons for investing resources in the training and education of all workers – in order to improve their productivity – many policies were directed at the long-term unemployed, with the aim of equipping the unemployed with the appropriate skills they need to find work. Youth Training Schemes and Job Training Schemes for young workers date back to the early 1980s. 'Restart' and similar training and re-skilling programmes targeted at the unemployed, with varying degrees of success have also proved a major element in the government's response to persistent mismatches of supply and demand in the labour market. In addition the UK government in the early 1990s introduced a number of other initiatives to reduce the deficiencies in the labour market. These included the setting up of **Training and Enterprise Councils** (TECs) which were charged with meeting the training, enterprise and vocational education requirements of local communities and employers. Similarly, the Technical and Vocational Educational Initiative (TVEI) was introduced in the early 1990s to influence the whole curriculum of schools and colleges in the preparation of 14–18 year olds for work. In addition there was the development of Investors in People which through the TECs attempted to set 'national' standards of training whilst the National Training Awards scheme was introduced to reward organisations publicly for their good practice.

The Labour administration has, in many respects, carried on these schemes and introduced others such as the New Deal and Welfare to Work programmes (see earlier). As a means to encourage lifelong learning, the Labour administration also introduced the new Individual Learning Account. The ILA is a savings account which individuals can use to build up money to pay for training courses. The government also replaced the TECs with the Learning and Skills Council (LSC).

The result of all these programmes has served to improve labour mobility; nonetheless mobility is still hampered because some areas of the workforce lack the appropriate skills. International comparisons with other major European countries show that the UK still lags behind though there are some indications that the gap is narrowing. In terms of basic skills, the International Literacy Survey carried out in 1997 showed that Britain came tenth out of twelve participating countries in terms of the numbers of people with inadequate levels of literacy. This lack of even basic skills clearly puts the brake on the performance of organisations. Poor literacy also hampers job mobility. Skills deficiencies span all levels from basic skills through generic skills, intermediate and managerial skills. In fact many of the improvements that have been made have occurred at the younger age level, 19–21 years of age, and it will take many years before the skills gap and skills shortages are removed from the whole of the workforce.

Geographical mobility

One of the major impediments to job mobility from regions where unemployment is relatively high is the higher cost of private housing. Approximately 70 per cent of families now live in their own homes, forcing them to buy and sell if they are to take jobs in other regions. Although the slump in the housing market between 1988 and the early 1990s hit the south-east hardest, reducing the size of the 'north-south' price differential, there has been a widening again of the differential following the more subdued boom of the late 1990s and the early part of the new millennium. The average house price in London in October 2000 is £145,104 whilst the average price in the North of England is £56,228. In addition, for a number of households, there is the problem of negative equity which also prevents them from moving, even though building societies and banks have come up with ingenious schemes to help people out of this problem.

For those in rented accommodation, long waiting lists make it very difficult to obtain council housing in a new area. The setting up of a Tenants' Exchange Scheme and a National Mobility Office were designed to assist geographical mobility, but it remains restricted due to high house prices in the south-east, cuts in local authority housing programmes and the continued absence of a significant private rented sector.

Wages councils and minimum wages

In many non-unionised sectors of the economy, earlier governments had previously established 'wages councils' to enforce minimum wages, in the belief that employers would otherwise exploit their relative bargaining power by paying unacceptably low wages. The Conservative government in the early 1990s argued that such agencies

Contrary to earlier fears, the impact of the national minimum wage has been benign, yet a question remains over its implementation.

It might seem premature to celebrate the national minimum wage just over six months since its introduction. But when the Low Pay Commission, the government-appointed body which determined the rate at which it was set, meet today they might be forgiven for feeling pleased with themselves.

It is true that the full impact of the minimum wage will only become apparent over a complete economic cycle, including the troughs when the extra payroll costs to employers may not be so easy to absorb. For now, though, the signs are encouraging.

Business leaders and the Tories warned that a statutory wage floor would lead to widespread job losses and an upsurge in inflation. Contrary to this, however, the labour market is flourishing and prices are rising at their slowest rate for 36 years. Office for National Statistics data show that the number of people in work hit a record high of more than 27m in the latest quarter. Economists say there is a very real prospect of unemployment falling below 1m next year.

Cynics may say the reason the impact of the minimum wage has been benign at the macroeconomic level is that it was set too low to make any difference. (It is £3.60 an hour for adults; £3, rising to £3.20 next June, for 18–21 year olds.) But try telling that to the estimated 1.9m people who have enjoyed a pay rise averaging 30 per cent as a result of the legislation.

In distributional terms the effect has been significant. Evidence shows the biggest narrowing in the hourly pay gap between men and women since 1991, largely due to the minimum wage. The minimum wage meant a 4.8 per cent increase in pay for workers in the personal and protective services, which include chefs, cleaners, bar staff, hairdressers, care workers and security guards.

In defiance of the predictions of the staunch free marketeers, there does not appear to have been a damaging knock-on effect on differentials higher up the pay scale.

Mark Atkinson, adapted from 'Minimum fuss',
The Guardian, 15 October 1999

produced similar distortions to trade unions, tending to raise minimum wages in line with prices, but responding slowly to downward pressure on prices and company profits during recessionary periods. For this reason, they abolished wage councils in August 1993. With the abolition of wages councils, Britain became the only EU country without any formal or informal system of minimum wages.

The election of the Labour administration in 1997 saw the signing up to the Social Charter and the introduction of national minimum wage (NMW). Both, it could be argued, would lead to increased rigidities in the labour market. One reason why the NMW may not have such detrimental effects on the labour market and UK competitiveness is that it affects sectors which are mostly in the service sector and not directly involved with exports. In addition, the NMW for adults was set at £3.60 an hour in April 1999 rising to £3.70 in October 2000, with a lower level set for workers under the age of 21. These levels were considered to be at the low end of the scale and perhaps did not increase wage costs in a major way. For example, the £3.60 approximated to 55 per cent of median hourly earnings in the UK and around 45 per cent of median hourly earnings for full-time males. The current rate is also lower than that in France though it is higher than that in the US. Initial evidence suggests that the NMW has had little adverse effect on the economy. A CBI survey in October 1999 showed that only 10 per cent of businesses considered the minimum wage as having a negative impact. One positive impact has been the narrowing of the hourly pay gap between men and women; furthermore, it does not seem to have had any knock-on effect on differentials further up the scale. However, are we seeing just short-term effects at this stage? The NMW has been introduced when the UK economy is growing at a promising rate and jobs during this period are continually being created. The long-term effect of an NMW may need to be considered over the whole economic cycle.

Conclusions

A flexible, efficient labour force is clearly crucial for a successful supply-side. There is little doubt that, before 1979, the British labour market was excessively rigid, plagued by poor industrial relations, and subject to unrealistic attitudes to pay and performance. The trade union reforms initially undertaken by successive Conservative administrations between 1979 and 1997, and against strong opposition from the Labour movement, have not been dismantled by the new Labour administration. Further areas of Labour reform have also been carried out by the current government, not least of which are the introduction of more flexible working arrangements, a raft of family friendly policies, the signing of the Social Charter and the introduction of the NMW.

Although a number of schemes have been introduced to promote occupational and geographical mobility, aimed at reducing the natural rate of unemployment, there still remain structural rigidities in the UK labour market. In particular, the UK is still subject to skill shortages and the poor standard of training and education suggest that Britain still faces serious, and as yet unresolved, problems in terms of the quality of its labour force.

KEY WORDS

New Deal
Minimum wage
National Insurance
Working-tax credit
Child-care tax credit
Uniform Business Rate
Poll tax
State Earnings Related Pensions Scheme
Jobseeker's Allowance
Welfare to Work

Working Time Directive
Closed shop
Social Charter
Flexibility of the labour market
Labour mobility
Functional flexibility
Natural rate of unemployment
Training and Enterprise Councils
Wages councils

Further reading

Beherrell, A. (1997), 'What are supply-side policies? How can they be used to reduce unemployment?', *Economics Today*, Vol. 4, No. 4, pp.9–12.

Dillow, C. (2000), 'Minimum wage myths', *Economic Affairs*, Vol. 20, No. 1, pp.47–52.

Dolton, P. (1998), 'Old problem, New Deal', *Economic Review*, Vol. 16, No. 1, pp.24–26.

Lawell, F.M., (2000), 'Does the natural rate of unemployment still exist?, *Economics Today*, Vol. 7, No. 4, pp.6–10.

Romer, S. (1998), 'How important is the mobility of labour? Can the government improve it?', *Economics Today*, Vol. 5, No. 3, pp.2–4.

Smith, S. (2000), 'The minimum wage', *Economic Review*, Vol. 18, No. 1, pp.16–17.

Useful websites

TransAtlantic Information Exchange Service: http://www.tiesweb.org/
work/current_problems
Bank of England: http://www.bankofengland.co.uk/wplist.htm
DFEE: http://www.dfee.gov.uk/skillsforce

Note

[1]Union density is defined as the percentage of employed workers eligible for membership of a trade union who actually exercise their right and join a union.

Essay topics

1. (a) Explain why, if left to market forces, training is likely to be under-consumed.   [8 marks]
   (b) Assess three government policy measures to increase the quality of training.   [12 marks]
2. (a) Explain why labour may be geographically and occupationally immobile.   [8 marks]
   (b) Assess three government policy measures to increase the occupational mobility of labour.   [12 marks]

Data response question

This task is based on a question set by Edexcel in 1998.

Changing product and labour markets

In October 1978, when a Labour leader last addressed his party conference as Prime Minister, 235,000 people worked in Britain's collieries and 150,000 in its steel mills. Besides the mines and steelworks, the railways, power, gas and telephones (then part of the General Post Office) were state-owned. The Prime Minister, James Callaghan, was in deep political trouble. Not only did he head a minority government but a key economic policy, of keeping pay rises to below 5 per cent, was rejected by the party conference, as it had been by the Trades Union Congress the month before. The 'winter of discontent', electoral defeat and 18 years in opposition lay ahead.

Contrast all this with the prospect facing Tony Blair when he addresses his party conference next week. His parliamentary majority is so big that it is scarcely worth counting. Mr Blair dictates to the unions, not they to him. Just as striking are the changes in the economy since Labour last held office. The miners, crushed by the strike of 1984–85 (and the electricity industry's switch to burning gas), now number a mere 17,300. Only 36,500 work in steel mills, although the industry makes more than 80 per cent of what it did in the late 1970s. And the mines, steelworks and utilities are, of course, in private hands.

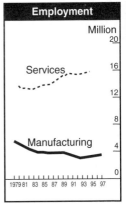

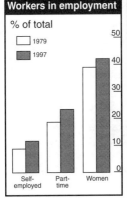

Privatised companies	
Quoted top 10	
Rank in FTSE 100	
British Petroleum	1
BT	7
Cable & Wireless	18
BG	20
British Aerospace	34
British Airways	37
National Power	40
BAA	42
Scottish Power	50
PowerGen	55

Striking, too, is the transformation of Labour's attitude to economic change. The party spent most of its time in opposition decrying the Conservatives' economic reforms. Not New Labour, and not Mr Blair. By and large he seems not merely to accept his economic inheritance, but to welcome it. Indeed, far from wanting to turn back the clock, Mr Blair says that he wants to speed it up. Mr Blair accepts that while Labour was out of office, Britain's economy changed irreversibly (see charts above).

'Design alone,' Mr Blair said in a recent speech, 'employs more than 300,000 people in Britain, more than in the car industry, let alone in traditional industries like shipbuilding or coal'. These days Britons are less likely to be trade unionists.

And then there are privatisation and deregulation. Of the firms in the FTSE 100 Index, 20 were publicly owned when Labour last left office. Even less thinkable for Old Labour, large chunks of the electricity and water industries are owned by foreign companies. Mr Blair's government no longer promises to reverse privatisation. It may even extend it.

It is not only Britain that has changed; the world has too. New Labour's fondness for talking about globalisation may be partly because it provides a politically acceptable way to ditch old ideas — 'it was not that we were wrong, you see, it's just that times have changed'. But it is true that since Labour was last in power economies around the world have become more open, not only to goods but to flows of capital.

Adapted from *The Economist*, 27 September 1997.

(a) Examine the economic causes of the changing number of trade union members in Great Britain. [10 marks]
(b) How might recent changes in Britain's employment patterns be explained? [20 marks]
(c) To what extent have privatisation and deregulation increased the competitiveness of British industry in recent years? [20 marks]

Chapter Six

Increasing investment innovation

'Measuring our progress in building a successful knowledge-driven economy is essential.'
Stephen Byers, Secretary of State for Trade and Industry, 2000

Introduction

Investment plays a critical role in the growth and development of an economy. However, investment, particularly business investment, is subject to large variations. Governments could operate a hands-off approach to private sector investment yet they often prefer to reduce perceived market failure through tax breaks and capital grants. What appears to be evident is that the UK under-invests both at a business level and at government level. This is not only in new capital goods but also in the area of R&D. There are some sectors that do well but the picture is further clouded by the fact that foreign firms undertake a high proportion of R&D in the UK. The UK also lags behind in the area of patents. Moreover, question marks can also be raised about UK organisations and their levels of innovation and imitation. Today, many governments see the knowledge economy as being the driving force behind further competitiveness in the global economy. It is not only the development of this knowledge but how receptive organisations are in using this knowledge that lies behind improvements in productivity and competitiveness.

Investment

Governments have adopted a number of approaches to raise the level of private sector investment. Some of these have been to fund industry directly, others have been to tie investment support into the various packages that make up government regional and industrial policy. Whether encouraged through **capital grants** or **tax breaks**, Table 9 shows that the components of business investment during the late 1990s have changed. Whereas total business investment and investment in services has grown in real terms between 1997 and 2000, total manufacturing sector investment has declined. In addition, since at least 1960 the UK has consistently invested less as a proportion of GDP than the OECD as a whole. The UK share has averaged approximately 18 per cent compared with the OECD average of almost 21 per

Table 9 Business investment, 1995 prices seasonally adjusted
(£ million)

		Total manufacturing	Construction and other production	Services	Public corporations non-manufacturing	Business investment
1997	Q4	4930	3416	15446	609	24401
1998	Q1	5334	3629	16087	575	25625
	Q2	5231	3560	16838	486	26116
	Q3	5077	3558	17583	533	26751
	Q4	5070	3856	17894	554	27374
1999	Q1	4564	2970	19952	564	28050
	Q2	4346	2859	20746	542	28493
	Q3	4281	2994	20696	558	28529
	Q4	4473	2854	20971	529	28827
2000	Q1	4672	2787	20921	411	28791
	Q2	4490	2455	21373	613	28931

Source: National Statistics, CSO, 2000.

cent. The UK has also invested out of a lower GDP per head, meaning a lower level of investment per worker. The UK has therefore a lower level of capital stock per worker and this helps explain why the UK's productivity is up to 40 per cent lower than some of its major competitors.

Tax relief versus capital grants

Governments have traditionally offered a range of incentives to encourage organisations to carry out investment plans and in doing so improve the supply-side of the economy. At an industry or firm level, government policy through tax relief on capital investments and business profits or via capital investment grants has been an important incentive. At the macroeconomic level, stability of the economy has also been important in determining investment, as have low interest rates. Determining which of the factors has the most important impact on private sector investment is difficult to ascertain. Some suggest that profits are of primary importance whilst others suggest that stop-go economic policies are the most relevant. More recent studies during the 1990s suggest that corporation tax changes and the loss of capital allowances have created a situation where organisations have reduced their own investments. Such changes during the 1990s were seen as equivalent to a permanent increase in interest rates of 2 per cent.

The process by which investment is encouraged has shifted over time. At the micro level the various governments since the Second World War have used a variety of **carrot and stick** methods to improve business investment. One approach adopted during the 1980s was through the setting-up of **Enterprise Zones**. These were areas into which organisations were attracted through tax and business rates relief; however, they were phased out during the 1990s because they were deemed to be an expensive way of creating jobs. The Regional Development Agencies (RDAs), set up in 1998, have again called for their re-introduction particularly with a focus on tax incentives for organisations within the zones as a means to stimulate investment. The RDA's view is that investment should be rewarded rather than the government taking the financial risks up front itself through grants.

During the late 1990s, New Labour have continued to provide a range of capital allowances especially for small firms to improve their investment performance. These allowances permit a company to write off more quickly the cost of buying new machinery against tax. However, not all firms are as efficient as others and giving them all (efficient and less efficient) capital allowances may prove to be a waste of resources in the long term as some of the less efficient firms will cease to operate in the market during tighter economic conditions. In 1999 a new £1 billion enterprise initiative was also developed to raise private sector investment. This was to use £245 million of government money to attract £755 million of funds from the private sector, designed to encourage investment especially in smaller companies and deprived regions.

Tax incentives for investment

Further help to improve investment performance was also developed in the budget of 2000 with capital gains tax reforms which would further strengthen the incentives for business to invest. Permanent 40 per cent first-year capital allowances for SMEs were introduced. An Enterprise Management Incentives (EMI) scheme followed in April 2000 to help recruitment and retention of key employees by small higher-risk companies by offering tax-advantaged share options. At the same time corporation tax starting rates were also reduced to 10 per cent.

Other methods to stimulate private sector investment have come through the setting up of Venture Capital Trusts (VCTs). These were created in 1995 to replace the Business Expansion Scheme and offer a range of tax breaks to investors. By 1999 they had channelled a total of £281 million into 312 companies. However, even here there are weaknesses, not least because the amount of money raised is far less than the £2.5 billion forecast. VCTs also tend to target larger organisations, which are less risky. They may not consider companies that only require small amounts of funding and those that require start-up or seed capital.

During the late 1990s the focus of support for investment shifted towards creating the conditions in which all businesses can survive, rather than pouring money into national champions or lame ducks. Emphasis was placed on improving productivity and raising the skills base through concentrating government policy on 'high quality knowledge-based projects'. However, the current Labour administration has still been forced to offer subsidies, where agreed with Brussels, to companies. For example, before BMW sold the Rover Group, the Labour government was willing to subsidise BMW with over £120 million of direct support along the lines of the direct support provided by the previous Conservative administration to Ford.

The general picture of the late 1990s is not the debate as to whether industry, through either regional or industrial policy, should receive support from either tax breaks or capital grants, but what sort of industrial policy should be followed. Pumping money into industry via grant aid, providing factory space and helping with training are not considered now to be the only ways to promote development and competitiveness.

Industrial policy

Industrial policy can be defined as the wide range of government actions designed to promote growth and increase the competitiveness of a particular sector or sectors of an economy. Traditional industrial policy instruments include macroeconomic and tax policies, subsidies for government procurement programmes, support to R&D, procedures for elaborating technical standards, education and infrastructure improvement programmes, favourable competition regimes, export assistance, and foreign trade and investment policies.

In Europe such policies have ranged from the 'dirigiste' policies of the French during the late 1960s through to the role of selective intervention or strategic industrial policy and on to the more Thatcherite non-interventionist policies. Market-based industrial policy is based on the notion that intervention by the state should only occur where there are significant features of market failure, for example significant under-provision of R&D. However, advocates of market-based industrial policies doubt whether the government can correct market failures successfully and some argue that governments might actually make the situation worse. Interventionalists, on the other hand, argue that left to its own devices the market fails to invest sufficiently in

R&D and that direct government intervention is required through either tax breaks or government grants. The strategic approach acknowledges that some governments have sought to pick winners and develop strategically important national or regional industries.

Changing nature of industrial policy

At a national level the UK has veered between direct intervention adopted post-Second World War and the more market-based approaches that have operated since 1979. The policy tools supporting industries in these areas generally operated in two ways. First, they involved financial incentives to firms located in or moving to, those areas; and second, the scope of development outside the areas was limited through the control of Industrial Development Certificates (IDCs). The policy instruments that have been used historically included financial assistance through Regional Development Grants. These were stopped in 1988 when the view was that some regions were becoming over-dependent on this type of funding. Since then, the shift has been to Regional Selective Assistance (RSA), a discretionary grant that can be either administered as a capital-related grant or job-related grant. Critics argue that RSA has not been very useful in attracting well-paid, skilled and economically resilient jobs. Moreover, capital intensive or high value-added investment projects have been bypassing the UK because RSA is job-related and fails to provide the level of fiscal incentives to match those offered by other European countries. Others, however, argue that since the 1970s, although the RSA grants have cost billions, it has created jobs, albeit expensive ones and the loss of this support could see job creation leap-frogging the more northern regions of the UK. However, support of this type has not prevented the closure of some high-profile state-aided plants such as those by Siemens and Fujitsu.

For organisations outside Assisted Areas, Regional Investment Grants (RIGs) are available and these are supplemented for the whole of the UK by other grants from the EU through its structural funds, ERDF, ESF and Agricultural and Fisheries Support. Small firms have been supported through the Small Business Service, which it was hoped would boost innovation. Extra direct funding has also been developed to help small manufacturing firms bring their ideas to the market, and support their R&D. Tax breaks have also been developed to encourage experienced managers to join high-risk companies.

EU industrial policy

At the same time as industrial policy was being developed and changed within the nation state, the EU was also beginning to develop its own industrial policy. There was much debate in Europe during the 1970s and 1980s as to what should be the direction of EU industrial policy. By the 1990s the EU set forth its industrial policy which opted for a middle way, not a top-down dirigiste policy but 'anything but a policy of laissez faire'. In spite of the references to **subsidiarity**, EU policy sharply limited the scope of national industrial policies and reflected a middle way between a philosophy of emphasis on equity (regulation of markets to protect a range of interests) and efficiency (an unfettered, integrated market).

EU **industrial policy** has concerned itself with areas like European deregulation, such as in telecoms, banking, etc, **state aids** to industry, privatisation, public procurement and actively encouraging the development of national champions. The EU has also supported the SME sector through a variety of measures since this was the sector that was deemed to be the driving force behind growth within the union. In the 1990s the Commission's focus has moved to developing industrial policy in a horizontal fashion believing in establishing greater competitiveness amongst European enterprises. There have also been movements to encourage industries within the EU to make greater use of IT. In particular in the area of R&D, the EU developed the Fourth Framework Agreement which ran between 1994 and 1998 which had as one of its goals the need to raise the international competitiveness of European industries and increase the spin-offs from European research. At the same time the EU has recognised the importance of innovation for EU industry if it is to become effective against the growth of international competitiveness.

Research and development

R&D has a number of beneficial effects on an economy. It can lead to:

- spotting, opening up and developing new market opportunities;
- creating new and more competitive products, services and processes;
- creating high-quality employment opportunities for 'high value-added' skilled people.

Table 10 shows how gross expenditure on R&D changed between 1990 and 1998.

In 1998 the UK's gross expenditure on R&D in money terms was £15.5 billion, representing an increase in money terms of 5 per cent over

Table 10 Gross expenditure on R&D in the UK (£ million)

	In money terms	In real terms (1995 prices)	Money terms per cent of GDP
1990	11,991	14,097	2.13
1991	12,131	13,429	2.06
1992	12,689	13,597	2.07
1993	13,541	14,135	2.09
1994	14,046	14,455	2.05
1995	14,172	14,172	1.96
1996	14,470	14,018	1.96
1997	14,758	13,906	1.81
1998	15,548	14,188	1.81

Source: Office for National Statistics, CSO, 2000.

the 1997 figure. However, since 1993 the expenditure on R&D as a proportion of GDP has fallen. Consideration of the expenditure on R&D by sector reveals that in 1998, 65.8 per cent came from business enterprises, 19.6 per cent from higher education and 9.6 per cent from the government. Overall the government funded 31 per cent of all R&D in the UK (25 per cent of civil R&D and 63 per cent of defence R&D). However, compared to the average for G7 countries, UK government spending per worker fell in real terms between 1985 and 1995. In addition only one of the world's top fifty corporate research investors was a UK company in 1998 and once the figures are adjusted for population, the Netherlands, Canada, France and the US had four times as many such companies, Germany and Japan five and Switzerland 25 times as many.

Britain is not alone in showing a decline in nominal expenditure on R&D as a proportion of GDP; however the decline in the UK is the steepest. Partly this can be explained by the result of the 'peace dividend' as expenditure by governments on defence R&D was reduced and the reclassification of the Atomic Energy Authority to the business sector in the late 1980s. This is not to say that R&D expenditure in some areas such as pharmaceuticals is not up there with the best, but areas such as metal products, machinery and equipment have undertaken relatively low levels of R&D compared with international standards. The OECD suggests that the reason why a number of countries have performed better in the area of R&D compared with the UK is that their incentives are more generous than those in the UK. In some instances they give tax relief for more than 100 per cent of R&D spending and subsidise its cost.

The government has begun to recognise the importance of government-financed R&D on the knowledge base of the economy and has allocated a further £1.4 billion of government funding between 1999 and 2002. This may be most apposite since some believe there is a strong link between government R&D and industry R&D. In addition the system of tax credits for R&D was expanded in 1999, cutting the minimum qualifying threshold of company spending from £50,000 to £25,000, and raising the turnover ceiling from £11.2 million to £25 million. The relief on R&D spending was also raised in April 2000 to 150 per cent. This is claimable even if there are no tax profits, and even if the trade has not yet started. As such the R&D tax credit system which will cost £150m a year will underwrite almost one-third of R&D costs for small business.

Business R&D

Business R&D is the largest component of overall R&D. In 1999 the UK's largest companies invested as much in R&D as their foreign competitors, but this was not true for all UK companies as a whole. In particular since 1981, the performance of UK firms has worsened, especially *vis-à-vis* the US and Japan. Even taking into account sectoral differences, the UK performs less well in most areas with only drugs and metal products matching international R&D levels. Low levels of R&D affect organisation competitiveness. It could disadvantage UK firms in that they are unable to develop, or identify new technologies which have commercial applications and without high levels of R&D, UK organisations may become stuck in familiar markets where they are increasingly under pressure from low cost competition.

The innovation process

The whole process involving R&D and investment, the way resources are made available to the knowledge economy and are then transformed into outcomes resulting in higher productivity and greater wealth, has been termed the 'innovation process'. This measure of a nation's innovative capacity includes more than just investment and R&D expenditure and should consider the openness of an economy to foreign ideas, the extent of collaboration and interaction between firms and between firms and the science base, and the degree of dynamism and entrepreneurship in the economy. The UK appears to have weaknesses in a number of areas of the innovation process, especially business spend on innovation/R&D by the manufacturing sector, though not by services; the UK's patenting performance and in the area of university spin-outs.

A Study says Britons work longer hours for less pay, have poor basic skills and have no enterprise culture.

Unveiling an in-depth audit of Britain's strengths and weaknesses, Mr Byers has stressed that action to remedy a range of weaknesses will depend on business as well as government.

'We have a long-hours culture, but we are not getting the rewards for it,' Mr Byers said.

He said that indicators would be used to monitor the progress of the UK as a knowledge-driven economy, to assess Britain's competitiveness and to help in the design of policies to narrow the gap in productivity and living standards.

According to the data collected by the Department of Trade and Industry, national income per head is 18 per cent below the average for the group of seven industrial nations, largely due to the much higher living standards in the USA.

There are some positive aspects for the UK economy, including the prospects for economic stability, our openness to international trade and investment, the fact that our labour market is regarded as functioning well, and our strong science base.

'But it is not all good news. We are poor on innovation, have poor basic skills, don't have a culture of enterprise, there are not enough spin-offs from universities and we don't have strong and confident consumers.'

Mr Byers added that it would be six or seven years before the results of supply-side changes were evident, but that the indicators would be published each year as a benchmarking exercise.

Britain's recent strong employment growth has been at the expense of weak productivity growth, but the Industry Secretary said there was no innate reason why the economy should not get the best of both worlds. 'But this is a wake-up call for business,' he said. 'There are weaknesses which we have to tackle.'

Management needs to improve if Britain is to be a successful knowledge economy. 'There is a shortage of good managers, particularly for fast-growing companies in high-technology sectors,' he added.

The DTI says UK consumers don't complain enough when they receive poor quality goods and services. 'Discerning and informed consumers are an important spur to competition and innovation ... Anecdotal evidence suggests UK consumers show more inertia and are generally less demanding than in other countries.'

Larry Elliott, Economics Editor, adapted from 'Byers tells business to shape up', *The Guardian*, 13 December 1999

The importance of business expenditure on R&D has been noted above, but innovation spending would include elements of money spent on design, training, marketing and equipment that are linked to the development of innovative new products or processes.

One approach used to judge the success of innovation is to look at the revenue generated by new or improved products. On the basis of considering products introduced between 1994 and 1996, UK manufacturers are in the bottom half of the EU league in terms of revenue they earn from new or improved products. Only 23 per cent of turnover is derived from these products compared with an EU average of 31 per cent. Thus UK manufacturers have a greater dependency on revenue generated from older products. So although a greater proportion of manufacturers describe themselves as innovators, the low level of innovation spending appears to lead to relatively low levels of earnings from product innovation.

External R&D

Part of business R&D expenditure in the UK also comes from foreign firms resident in the UK. Greater internationalisation of R&D should enhance the capacity of the host economy if they can access the global pool of knowledge and so keep pace with technology leaders.

The share of UK R&D accounted for by foreign organisations is one of the highest in the OECD. Between 1985 and 1996 the share rose by two-thirds, partly reflecting the takeover of R&D establishments by foreign companies. This augers well for the UK in the sense that foreign firms are attracted to the UK for their R&D because of the strong science and engineering base of the UK. In addition they bring new forms of technologies and organisational methods which can diffuse throughout the UK economy. However, many of these research centres may have little to do with the company's operating subsidiaries, thus these organisations may not benefit greatly from increased foreign R&D.

If UK organisations are more reticent about undertaking R&D themselves, one way forward is for them to gain access to international R&D through **technological alliances**. There is evidence to suggest that UK firms enter into more international technological alliances compared with other EU countries and this may enable them to gain their competitive edge. Although technology transfer between firms and economies is important, productivity improvements can come through imitation and these may be a far more important source of improvements for the economy. Therefore UK and European receptiveness to new technologies, and the capacity to assimilate them, has been as important as inventiveness itself.

Developing patents

Patents are also very important in the context of R&D. The patent system is needed to protect an inventor and thereby address the degree of market failure. Although the patent may give monopoly power to the inventor, the benefits to society from the invention should outweigh the costs to society. It is arguable as to whether the patent system itself yields for the inventor as much return as that which can arise from the value of trade secrets, know-how, name recognition, service capabilities and the like. Moreover, are patents really that valuable when history shows many examples where organisations have sat on patents and where other organisations have got round the original patent? Conversely, there is the view that patents are important as an indication of inventiveness and entrepreneurial activity and improving the number of patents registered by a country is an important feature that lies behind the whole growth process.

For the government the amount of patents is one measure of invention and dynamism of the economy, albeit a flawed one, since not all inventions are patented. For example, patenting is rarely used in the software sector, one of the areas of strongest growth in recent years. Patents are also of unequal value, some cover very low value inventions whilst others cover major technological and commercial successes. In comparing the numbers of patents within different countries it needs to be noted that different countries have different patenting systems so it is more useful to consider the patents by country within particular markets such as the US or EU. Looking at patents filed within the EU and US, the UK underperforms compared with the US and Japan and more particularly is worse than both Germany and France though somewhat better than Italy. Therefore the UK has some way to catch up with a number of its major competitors.

To help with the cost of patenting, patent application fees were abolished in 1998 and the cost of UK Patent Office fees were reduced by 20 per cent giving annual savings to industry of £12 million. However, there is still much to do, not least the introduction of an affordable and easy to enforce EU patent, the requirement of an international treaty on patents and the development of a 'first to file' system with the USA.

Capital market developments

Investment in R&D and innovation often depends on the availability of finance. One area of capital market reform has been to address the difficulties organisations face with regard to insufficient funding for their capital expenditure programmes. On one level this is due to an **equity gap** existing, particularly for **small and medium-sized enterprises**, but even for larger firms there may also be a shortage of long-term bank finance. Having long-term interest rates that are currently at their lowest for a number of years are of little use if banks will not lend to businesses. If banks will not lend to organisations then one possibility is a substantial tax allowance for capital investment. Some have even argued for the development of an industrial development bank. Conversely, it has been argued that the failure of British banks to supply sufficient amounts of capital for British firms is an illustration of an efficient capital market compared with those in continental Europe, since they are more likely to drive poor performers out of business by withholding funds.

Both capital markets in the EU and the UK must work effectively to provide a range of flexible funding for investment. Banks and trade finance are the most important sources of finance for the majority of smaller firms. Where projects are conceived as being of high risk or where returns are long term, equity finance may be more appropriate. Venture capital both for start up and the early stages of growth is therefore important. In the UK, the growth of venture capital as a source of equity finance for smaller firms grew until 1990, collapsed somewhat during the recession in the early 1990s but has grown substantially since then. The growth of the venture capital industry leads to important knowledge spillovers into the economy giving both static and dynamic effects. To recognise the importance of venture capital, an Enterprise Fund was created in 1998 and there have been tax incentives put in place to encourage the development of this market.

European venture capital markets

Europe too, needs a strong venture capital market similar to that which has developed in the US. For example, the US has a bigger equity market. In Europe, the equity market is 32 per cent of GDP, while in the US it is 68 per cent. Once established through the use of venture capital, venture capitalists may wish to cash in their investments. The lack of a vibrant venture capital market may deter them from making the initial investment. In this respect the UK and Europe have developed a number of exchanges which help facilitate the buying and selling of shares such as AIM, EASDAQ and Euro NM. However, when compared with the NASDAQ and NASDAQ Small Cap markets in the US, the UK and European offering are some way behind and this failure to have a well-developed venture capital market may limit the growth of some UK and European companies. For larger companies this is not as great an issue. The London Stock Exchange was the fourth largest market in the world by capitalisation in 1998 behind New York, NASDAQ and Tokyo. However, being large may not be sufficient since capital markets need to be efficient and innovative.

Savings gap

In addition to improving capital markets in general, governments have sought to improve the **savings ratio** in an attempt to improve the availability of funds that can be channelled into investment. In 1999 individual savings accounts (ISAs) were introduced to encourage saving, especially by lower income groups. These were to replace personal equity plans (PEPs) which tended to be taken out by higher income groups. Both are ways of making tax-free savings. Critics have argued that ISAs are too complex for new savers and that the individuals buying into these are not really low income groups. The replacement of PEPs and tax exempt savings accounts (TESSAs) by ISAs is likely to result in a reduction in the overall level of national wealth by around 4 per cent of GDP since there is a reduced limit on the amount of funds that can be invested in an ISA in any one year.

In addition to ISAs and PEPs governments have tried to increase the base of UK share ownership. Share ownership grew through the privatisation process in the UK but governments have also encouraged share ownership through approved profit-sharing schemes (APS), the SAYE scheme and the discretionary share option scheme. All provide tax incentives for employees to buy shares in their companies.

Conclusion

The McKinsey Institute pointed out that productivity in the UK could be improved through increasing investment and innovation. In seeking to do this governments have used a variety of measures. Grants have been used to encourage firms to expand or to attract both domestic and overseas firms into specific geographical areas or products. Alternatively, governments have offered tax breaks to organisations. Their scope for offering both these types of incentives is partially limited by European regulations on state aid and the like. In addition governments have tried to encourage investors to invest more to reduce the equity gap faced by organisations whilst at the same time encouraging more saving which can be channelled into investment. Many of these policies have been expensive and their impact on businesses and UK productivity has not always been clear. Moreover, there are still concerns about the level of R&D and the degree to which this is not commercially related or cannot be spun off into commercial ventures. At least governments have come to recognise the problems of under-investment. The improvements that have been made to address some of the failures of the supply-side are unlikely to be seen in the short term and it may be some time before improvements in R&D, innovation and imitation will close the gap between the UK and its major competitors.

KEY WORDS

Capital grants
Tax breaks
Carrot and stick
Enterprise Zones
Industrial Policy
Dirigiste policies
Subsidiarity
State aids

Innovation process
Technological alliances
Patents
Equity gap
Small and medium-sized
  enterprises
Savings ratio

Further reading

Bloom, N. (1999), 'Tax Relief and R&D', *Economic Review*, April, pp.16–17.

Curwen, P. (1997), 'Does the UK have an industrial policy?', *Economics Today*, March, pp.5–8.

The Economist (1996), 'The road from imitation to innovation', 18 May, p.102

Ingham, A. (1998), 'Investment subsidies: a political card worth playing?, *Economic Review*, February, pp.31–33.

Kealey, T. and Al-Ubaydli, (2000), 'Should governments fund science?', *Economic Affairs*, September, pp.4–9.

Useful websites

Cabinet Office: www.cabinet-office.gov.UK/

Supply-side economics: www.citinv.it/associazioni/NEP/polec-ita/0154. html

DTI: www.dti.gov.UK/comp/competitive/ec_ch1.htm

National Competitiveness Council: www.forfas.ie/report/ncc99/comp. htm

Essay topics

1. 'Taiwan to invest £1 billion in the UK.' (*The Sunday Times*, 15 March 1998)
   (a) Analyse the factors which Taiwanese companies would take into consideration before building new manufacturing facilities in the UK. [40 marks]
   (b) Examine the likely economic effects of such investments on:
       (i)   the UK's balance of payments;
       (ii) aggregate demand and aggregate supply in the UK. [60 marks]

[Edexcel, Paper 2, Q6, June 1999].

2. (a) Explain what factors influence the level of innovation in a country. [8 marks]
   (b) Discuss three supply-side policies which could be implemented to increase the level of innovation in a country. [12 marks]

Data response question
This task is based on a question set by OCR in 1997.

Wages inequality within and between countries

Figure A: Global labour supply (wages in US$ at 1992 prices)[1]

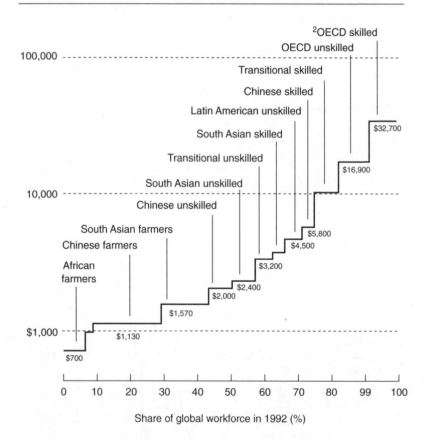

Share of global workforce in 1992 (%)

Notes

1   Wages are given as average figures for the specific groups shown. For example, African farmers earn on average US$700 per year. Vertical distances between average wage levels, represent equal percentage differences rather than equal absolute differences.

2   The Organisation for Economic Co-operation and Development (OECD) is made up of the 25 major industrial countries in the world including the United States, Japan, Germany and the UK.

There is substantial inequality in wage levels both within and between countries. At the bottom of the global labour supply are hard-working peasants making up over 40 per cent of the world's labour force of around 3.5 billion. They subsist on average wages (measured in common international prices) of less than US$1 600 per year. Towards the other end, on about US$17 000 per annum, are the unskilled workers of the major industrialised countries, a relatively privileged 8 per cent of the global workforce.

There is, however, some dispute as to the main explanation for the growing wage inequality within many of the rich countries of the OECD. Some suggest that the growth in international trade with countries from lower wage developing areas, like South Asia or China, can explain almost entirely the decline in the relative living standards of unskilled workers in OECD countries such as the UK. Others believe that a more likely explanation for the relative changes in the demand for labour in high income countries is rapid technological advance. This gives those who have the appropriate skills a considerable advantage.

1. (a) (i)   Use Figure A to identify the main features of global wage inequality between different types of worker.   [2 marks]

   (ii)   Use the information provided to identify **one** feature of inequality in average wages between different countries.
   [1 marks]

   (iii)   State **two** of the problems involved in using average wages in US $ at 1992 prices as the basis for a comparison of average **incomes** between workers in different countries.   [2 marks]

   (b) (i)   From the data in Figure A, explain why there might be rural-urban migration in China.   [2 marks]

   (ii)   Identify and explain **one** problem that might arise from extensive rural-urban migration.   [2 marks]

   (c)   Use the information provided to explain how trade between the UK and South Asia might affect unskilled workers in the UK.   [3 marks]

(d) (i)   What is meant by the occupational mobility of labour?
[1 mark]
   (ii) Explain how technological change can affect the occupational mobility of labour.   [2 marks]
   (iii) Discuss **one** possible policy that could be used to increase the occupational mobility of unskilled workers in the UK.   [5 marks]
2. Estimates of the overall elasticity of demand for labour with respect to the wage rate in the UK in the 1980s were given as -0.33 after one year, rising to -0.9 in the longer run.
   (a) Explain the meaning of these figures and describe the factors that influence the wage elasticity of demand for labour in the short run and the long run.   [10 marks]
   (b) Discuss the use that might be made of these wage elasticity of demand figures by trade union officials who are preparing to ask employers for a 5 per cent wage increase for all their union members throughout the country.   [10 marks]
3. 'Unless the burden of state-retirement pensions can be reduced, demographic changes throughout Europe will cause increasing resentment and a lack of incentive among taxpaying working people.'
   (a) Use indifference curves to explain how an individual's willingness and ability to work may be affected by an increase in direct tax rates.   [10 marks]
   (b) Discuss the range of policies which a government could adopt to deal with the problems of financing state retirement pensions.   [10 marks]

Chapter Seven

Promoting entrepreneurship

'The newest innovations – which we label information technologies – have begun to alter the manner in which we do business and create value, often in ways not readily foreseeable even five years ago.'
Alan Greenspan, Chairman US Federal Reserve Board, May 1999

Introduction

For many people, it is still large firms that dominate the financial pages and dominate markets. Yet after having ignored the small firm sector for most of the last century, governments came to realise that it was the small firm sector that was providing the growth in employment, were becoming more active in export markets and were important innovators. One subset of the small firms sector was also deemed to be of critical importance – that of high-technology small firms. These small firms were seen as the seed-bed of new ideas, and as the driving force behind improvements in productivity. Yet small firms generally and high-technology firms in particular were subject to a number of important constraints which limited their performance. Whilst governments during the 1980s and 1990s sought to help the small firm sector, there was a more rapid development which served to shake up the business world completely – the birth of the internet and development of e-commerce. Both are altering and will continue to alter competition in markets and shake-up business. Gaining a competitive advantage in the e-commerce world for their domestic organisations is one important role for governments in the new millennium.

The size of the SME sector

There were an estimated 3.7 million active enterprises in the UK at the start of 1998, a figure that has proved fairly consistent during the 1990s. The current figure of active enterprises has increased by over 50 per cent since 1980. At the same time there has been a similar increase in the number of self-employed businesses without employees which indicates that most of the growth has been in one-person businesses.

Of the 3.7 million enterprises at the beginning of 1998, 2.3 million were run by the self-employed and of the remaining firms, the vast majority were defined as small organisations (fewer than 50 employees). Only 25 000 were medium-sized enterprises (50–249 employees) and less than 7000 organisations could be considered large (250 or more employees).

If we examine the **small firms** sector more closely, it accounts for over 99 per cent of businesses in the UK, 45 per cent of non-government employment, and 38 per cent of turnover at the start of 1998. In contrast, the 7000 largest businesses accounted for 44 per cent of employment and 48 per cent of turnover. There are also important differences by industrial classification, as Table 11 indicates. In the construction industry more than two-fifths of the businesses had no employees, as was the case for education, whilst manufacturing, transport, financial intermediation and health and social work had a greater proportion of their workforces employed by larger businesses.

One important question to consider is whether small firms are different to large firms in their behaviour. If so, would an economy benefit from having a bigger smaller-firm sector which might boost the

Table 11 Size distribution of employment by industry: UK, 1998

Employment (000s)	100%	None	1–49	50–249	250+
All industries[1]	21,595	12.7	32.0	11.6	43.7
Agriculture, forestry and fishing	499	37.7	58.1	*	*
Mining and quarrying	87	5.7	*	*	*
Manufacturing	4,451	5.1	23.8	20.7	50.5
Electricity, gas and water supply	153	†	*	*	*
Construction	1,536	41.7	46.5	7.9	13.9
Wholesale, retail and repairs	4,423	7.4	36.5	9.4	46.7
Hotels and restaurants	1,570	4.6	45.1	8.7	41.6
Transport, storage, communication	1,487	12.3	19.2	8.3	60.2
Financial intermediation	1,026	4.8	11.0	7.1	77.1
Real estate, business activities	2,983	15.4	42.3	12.9	29.4
Education	240	41.7	27.1	*	*
Health and social work	2,063	9.3	25.1	8.1	57.5
Other social/personal services	1,075	28.7	38.7	9.3	23.2

Source: Labour Market Quarterly Report, DFEE, November 1999.

[1] The SME statistics exclude public administration, private households, extra-territorial bodies and labour recruitment and provision of personnel.

*Data suppressed to avoid disclosure.

†Less than 0.05 per cent.

country's competitiveness, the take-up of new ideas and improve over-all productivity? It is to these issues that we now turn.

Why are governments interested in the SME sector?

Large firms have often been seen as the engine of economic growth but over the last thirty years evidence has been accumulating to suggest that this may not be the case. This is due to a number of reasons:

- Large firms may not always be the most innovative – evidence was growing during the 1970s that small firms had an important role to play in innovation.
- The development of large firms was not always due to larger plants but through having a greater number of smaller plants.
- As large firms came into existence through external growth, the per-formance of newly merged firms often proved to be disappointing.
- Small firms appeared to be the job creators whilst it was large organisations which were reducing employee numbers.
- Small firms far from dealing with their domestic markets had become increasingly involved in international trade.
- During the 1990s, the annual average growth rate in the US exceeded that of Germany, France and the UK and the vibrancy of the US's small firms sector was seen as one of the important factors behind their relatively improved growth performance.
- Although Germany, Italy and Spain have more employment in the SME sector than the UK and US, it is the UK and US that have more very small firms than their continental European competitors and it is likely that these firms have the greatest growth potential.

Thus, because SMEs have been the job creators of the 1990s and are likely to be the same in the new millennium, have great growth poten-tial, are becoming increasingly internationally focused, are highly innovative, are less likely to be unionised and are more flexible, it is not surprising that governments see the SME sector as important.

Support for SMEs

Entrepreneurship in the UK is greater than in continental Europe, although not as high as in the US – one in 30 adults in the UK is trying to start a business, compared with one in 50 in France and Germany, but one in 12 in the US. Europe on the other hand shows a better per-formance in innovation. This suggests that potential output of the UK and other European economies could be expanded by improving the environment for business start-ups.

So what are the conditions which are perceived to enhance **entrepre-**

Support structures need a shake if they are to do the business

There are more than 200 different public sector programmes aimed at businesses and delivered through a variety of agencies – Business Links, Training and Enterprise Councils, Chambers of Commerce and so on. Yet in some areas of the country only minimal support is on offer to start-up companies despite evidence that new businesses – not only growing businesses – can help create different industries, can innovate, provide employment and regenerate stagnant communities.

That, according to the Institute for Public Policy Research, is why the Government must encourage entrepreneurship but must also reappraise and overhaul the current system of business support schemes.

The IPPR report on the Entrepreneurial Society recommends focused but significantly fewer central support services – down to nearer 20 from the more than 200 currently on offer. 'Myriad government support schemes have created a confusing and fragmented infrastructure.'

Appraisal of existing initiatives is poor. 'There is no coherent evaluation of programmes so mistakes are repeated and there is only haphazard development of a code of best practice.'

And it warns that the structures such as Business Link, through which schemes are delivered, must be fit for the purpose. 'If enterprise is about motivation, innovation and dynamism, then support agencies should incorporate some of these elements into their own design and promotion.'

The report highlights the importance of Government action in creating a supportive infrastructure. 'If we expect people to set up their own businesses, especially those without inherited money or those who do not own their own homes, then we can at least reduce some of the avoidable risk and create the right framework for potential success,' it says.

Undercapitalisation and failure to seek advice seem to be the most significant causes of the relatively low success rate of new firms.

Celia Weston, adapted from 'For entrepreneurship to work, planning and organisation is vital', *The Guardian*, 24 March 1998

neurship and the expansion of the small firms sector? One problem for UK SMEs is assumed to be access to finance.

Access to finance

Most UK small businesses are financed from retained profit, working capital, overdraft borrowing and owner's equity. Approximately 40 per cent of UK SMEs use loans, and 17 per cent have used external equity funding. SMEs are often reticent in using external funding because of loss of control; nonetheless, the percentage of UK SMEs using external funding is often higher than in other continental European countries. An area that has received much attention in the UK is the relationships between SMEs and banks. Often the rate of interest faced by SMEs is 2–5 per cent above the base rate since they are seen as higher risk investments. This perception of risk by banks appears to be based on a much more narrow profile in the UK who make greater use of financial statistics whereas some European banks in addition to financial variables use managerial information and consider the potential of the entrepreneur. In addition, UK banks have been criticised for not providing sufficient liquidity to avert bankruptcy unlike German banks. Moreover, because the banking system in the UK is dominated by national banks, the lack of regional banks reduces knowledge about the needs of particular localised industries. Finally, there have been questions raised about the short-termism of banks. This last factor has been challenged by a Bank of England report in 1998 which suggested that UK banks are equally as likely to lend long term to their domestic SMEs as European banks with their own SMEs. So how have governments helped with external funding in an attempt to fill the **equity gap** experienced by a number of SMEs?

- The Enterprise Investment Scheme (EIS): used to encourage equity investment in high risk SMEs, through the use of Business Angels who would offer capital and expertise and get tax relief on their investments.
- Loan Guarantee Scheme: introduced in 1981, the government acts as guarantor up to a maximum percentage, for a premium rate of interest for SMEs which are unable to provide sufficient collateral against a loan from a bank.
- Venture Capital Trusts (VCTs): introduced under the Finance Act 1995, the first twelve VCTs had raised £105m by April 1996. The trusts are exempt from capital gains tax, as are individuals who buy shares in a VCT.
- Alternative Investment Market (AIM): this, in many respects, replaced the Unlisted Securities Market (USM) which was wound-up in 1996. The AIM commenced in 1995 to meet the demand for low cost accessible investment for small and growing companies.

Outside of these schemes, **venture capital** has been seen to be one way to fill the equity gap experienced by SMEs. In the period 1993–98 venture capital investment in the UK increased threefold giving the UK the highest level of venture capital investment relative to GDP amongst European countries in 1998. However, the majority of UK venture capital is not used for business start-ups, but is used to fund management buy-outs or buy-ins. Thus the use of venture capital to fill the equity gap faced by UK start-ups is not really taking place. Moreover, the supply of venture capital to UK start-ups is also declining. This contrasts sharply with developments in Europe where the German Neuer market and French Nouveau Marché have been very successful in attracting smaller companies, boosting the attractiveness of venture capital investment.

Other small firm support

It is not only in the area of finance that governments have sought to address market failure in the SME sector. They have also attempted to boost the sector through allowances and grants. The corporation tax rate has been reduced on SME profits. Grants have been made available under the Enterprise Initiative for firms in development areas employing fewer than 25 people. Support for Products Under Research (SPUR) awards were available between 1991 and 1997 to help SMEs develop new products and processes which represent a significant technological advance. SMART (Small Firms Merit Award for Research and Technology) awards have been available since 1986 to promote technical or commercial feasibility studies into innovative technology.

In addition Small Firm Training Loans (SFTL) were introduced in 1996 for small firms up to 50 employees in order that a system of life-long learning could be established for their employees. These loans, between £500 and £125,000 are available from high street banks to help with training costs.

Apart from finance, tax allowances and grants, one further problem area constraining the performance of the small firm sector lies with advice and support for business problems.

Training and advice for SMEs

There are a number of features that have characterised **small business advice and support**:

- There exists an array of different providers of support that deliver a wide range of different schemes.
- There has been a lack of networking between the various support agencies.
- It has been difficult for SMEs to work out to which agencies they should turn to for specific advice.
- There are overlaps in support.
- The quality of provision from the different support agencies has differed.

- The support agencies have not always been proactive in contacting SMEs, developing relationships, and tailoring provision to the SME need rather than delivering national programmes.
- There has been a relatively low take-up of small business services from the support agencies.

The type of business support categorised by organisational status can be seen in Table 12. As we can see there are many sources to which SMEs can turn for business support, but the formulation of such support at both the national and local level is of vital importance.

Table 12 Types of business support organisation by organisational status

Public	Semi-public	Private	Other
Department of Trade and Industry	Business Links	Accountants	Managed workspaces
	Training and Enterprise Councils	Banks	Prince's Youth Business Trust
Department for Education and Employment		Solicitors	
	Department Companies	Venture capitalists	Livewire
Local Authority Economic Development Units	Universities	Local Enterprise Agencies	
	Further Education Colleges	Large corporate businesses	
Rural Development Commission		Private consultants	
Regional Development Agencies		Business angels	
		Private training organisations	
		Chambers of commerce	
		Small business representative groups	
		Trade associations	

Business Links

Business Links were launched in 1992 by Michael Heseltine as a one-stop shop to address the perceived market failure in the provision of advice and information, and the systems failure in small business support. Currently, there are 85 Business Links with a network of over 240 outlets. Although Business Links did provide SMEs with a focus for their support there were a number of issues with the Business Link concept and performance. There have been problems with accountability, turf wars have arisen with other providers and other business links and concerns have been raised over their financial viability since they are supposed to be self-financing. More importantly, there was some lack of penetration of the SME market by Business Links and they tended to focus on growth companies to the detriment of other SMEs. There was also a view that very small SMEs were not their target market and because Business Links needed to be income generators they competed with the private sector support agencies rather than complemented their activities. In addition, there were questions raised about the quality and the training of the personal business advisors.

Other government agencies developed to support the small business sector are the **Training and Enterprise Councils** (TECs). These were used to take forward the government's strategy for training in the 1990s. Developed in 1990, there are currently 81 TECs in operation. The TECs are independent companies run by boards of directors led by private sector business leaders and contracted by the government both to provide the whole country with a skilled workforce and to support and cordinate local economic development. In fact only 10 per cent of the TEC budgets have been used for the latter activity. In assessing the performance of the TECs a number of studies have noted the following:

- The provision of services has tended to be on a blanket basis without tailoring the services to the needs of the local community.
- There is still a lack of embededness within the local community.
- There is an image that the TECs are staffed by civil servants.
- Due to accountability issues and the fact that they encourage businesses to undertake training on a voluntary basis, TECs are considered as poorly run government agencies which have had little impact on unemployment.

SMEs and high-technology companies

While traditional economic sectors have been in decline over the last twenty years, expansion has occurred in technology-based fields and these 'new' sectors make an increasingly important economic contribution. It is understandable that at local, regional and national level government is eager to develop such companies as a means to improve competitive advantages, increase employment, and improve economic growth. To be able to improve the supply-side for high-technology SMEs requires an understanding of the characteristics of the **high-technology sector** so that market failures can be addressed.

The issues that face high-technology companies are extreme versions of problems facing SMEs in general. There are problems with start-up finance and with further development capital, with their abilities to manage technological transfer, whether entrepreneurs can protect their investment and ideas through the patent system and whether they need specific support infrastructure (such as a science park or incubator) to mature successfully.

With regard to finance, banks have been very reluctant to lend seed capital (money to develop ideas into prototypes) for risky high-technology projects. If entrepreneurs have difficulty in protecting their investment, then obtaining finance is also made harder. High-technology SMEs have become more reliant on venture capital but this, as we have seen earlier, is skewed towards management buy-outs or buy-ins. The government schemes such as SMART and SPUR may reduce some of the problems but they are often short term and not always easily available or promoted.

One approach to the supporting of high-technology companies is through the growth of science parks. Here clusters of small high-technology companies, often linked to a university, allow the SMEs to develop a wide range of networks within their close community. There is some disagreement as to whether science parks actually provide much benefit, however. Moreover, questions have been raised as to whether high-technology firms do have better growth performances.

New initiatives and small firms

The New Labour administration sought to address some of the constraints faced by high-technology SMEs.

- To improve the UK's enterprise culture, the government has worked with the British Chambers of Commerce to develop the National Campaign for Enterprise. Here a number of high profile business people will act as role models and mentors for young people.
- The government has introduced a new Enterprise Management Incentives (EMI) scheme to encourage people to join higher-risk companies, by offering tax-advantaged share options.
- The government has attempted to reduce the stigma attached to business failure.

- To encourage innovation, the Labour administration injected £1.4bn funds to ensure that the UK continues at the forefront of generating research.
- The government sought to increase university technology transfer through the development of the University Challenge Fund (£50m) and ran the Science Enterprise Challenge which provide £25m for eight centres of enterprise around the country.
- Early in 2000 the government also announced that the Massachusetts Institute of Technology (MIT) would jointly establish an Institute with Cambridge University, with the government providing £14m per year for 5 years to establish the Institute. The purpose of this is to develop technology-based business out of the academic base, develop a research programme in fields likely to have a substantial impact on the future evolution of technology, and undertake education and research designed to improve the UK's entrepreneurship, productivity and competitiveness.
- The government introduced in April 2000 an R&D tax credit to enable companies to offset some of the cost of R&D.
- The government intends to reform the planning system to strengthen the support for the growth and development of clusters of firms.

Many of these policy changes directed at the high-technology sector are recent and the full impact will only be noticed in the long term. At this stage they appear to be the first step in the right direction in improving the supply-side constraints faced by high-technology firms.

Internet and e-commerce

Although high-technology companies have been recognised as important in improving the growth performance and competitiveness of the UK economy, the rise of the **internet** and **e-commerce** will have more profound effects on competitiveness.

Electronic commerce lies at the heart of the government's vision for building a modern, knowledge-driven economy. The government's aim, as outlined in the 1998 Competitiveness White Paper is to 'make the UK the best environment in the world for e-commerce'. In the UK, e-commerce transactions in 1999 were worth around £2.8bn and they had the potential to grow ten-fold over the next three years, reaching approximately 4 per cent of total GDP by 2002. E-commerce will also have impacts on growth and inflation. Figures from the US Department of Commerce suggest that in the years 1995–98 the Information and Communications Technologies (ICT) industries – the important enablers of e-commerce – were responsible for 35 per cent of US real economic growth, whilst representing only 8 per cent of US GDP. In 1996 and 1997, these same industries were believed to have lowered US inflation by 0.7 per cent. Although the impact on employment is not quite as clear, the view is that if the UK fails to capitalise on the opportunities that e-commerce presents, then jobs and prosperity will be eroded by e-commerce competition from overseas.

Government policy and e-commerce
Despite a range of initiatives to promote e-commerce in the UK, the UK still lags behind the major economies of the US, Canada and Australia on measures of both business and consumer e-commerce use. In Europe, the UK is also substantially behind the smaller economies of Finland, Sweden and Norway. Germany and France are currently behind the UK but are taking large steps to improve their positions too.

The current government's plan is to make the UK the best environment in the world for e-commerce by 2002, and have set specific goals for individuals, business and government.

Compared with other G7 countries, for consumers it is envisaged that a higher percentage of people in the UK will have access to e-commerce networks from home, that the total cost of internet access will be lower in the UK, and a higher proportion of the population will use multi-function smart cards. For business, it is anticipated that a higher percentage of business-to-business and business-to-consumer transactions will be carried out on e-commerce networks than in any other G7 country, and for government, a higher proportion of total government services will be transacted through e-commerce networks than in any other G7 country.

However, there are barriers to this transformation needed for e-commerce.

- There is a lack of a clear, internationally agreed regulatory framework.
- Many companies do not understand the potential benefits and challenges that e-commerce can bring.
- There are also issues of access. Competition has driven down the price of PCs and software. OFTEL has plans to open the BT local access system to competitive use with new technologies.
- There are also the issues of trust. Consumers and businesses must be able to use e-commerce systems without undue fear of fraud.

Conclusions
Traditional patterns of working and traditional industries have never

been more under threat as we enter the new millennium. It may have taken governments some time to realise that although large organisations dominate markets it is the small firm sector which has an important role to play in innovation, improving competitiveness, and providing employment. As large companies have been shedding jobs it is the small firms sector which has been the provider of employment for many people. At the same time the small firm sector has suffered from market failure and has required government assistance in terms of tax breaks, reductions in regulatory red tape, and help with finance. Innovation does not appear to be a major deficiency with UK SMEs relative to continental Europe, yet creating an entrepreneurial environment is still a major weakness of the UK economy.

One group of SMEs, the high-technology sector, has also been singled out as an important driver behind possible productivity improvements in the UK economy, creating important spill-over effects into other areas of the economy. The jury still appears to be out as to whether high-technology companies are really that different from other SMEs. It is also felt that UK high-technology companies have missed a number of windows of opportunity in the past thus reducing their overall impact. In both the small firms sector generally, and the high-technology sector in particular, the new Labour government has sought to address some of the difficulties faced by these organisations.

Perhaps, though, the most important changes that are taking place in the global economy are in the area of the internet and e-commerce. The government realises the important of e-commerce and has set a number of challenging objectives for UK business and for government. If these are not met then other countries will once again achieve a competitive advantage over the UK.

KEY WORDS

Small firms	Training and Enterprise
Entrepreneurship	Councils
Equity gap	High-technology sector
Venture capital	Internet
Small business advice and	E-commerce
support	
Business Links	

Further reading

Cabinet Office (1999), *E-commerce @its.best.uk*, a Performance and Innovation Unit Report.

Department of Trade and Industry (1998), *Building the Knowledge Economy*, the 1998 Competitiveness White Paper, HMSO.

Greenbank, P. (1995), 'Small businesses: from growth to decline?', *EBEA Journal*, Vol. 3, Part 4, No.12, Winter.

Pipe, A. (1999), 'The importance of small firms', *Lloyds TSB Economic Bulletin*, London.

Walsh, J. (1998), 'Do small firms create jobs?', *Business Review*, Vol. 15, No. 2, Nov.

Useful websites

Cabinet Office: http://www.cabinet-office.gov.UK/innovations

Cordis: http://www.cordis.lu/export/src/smeframe.htm

Essay topics

1. (a) Assess the significance of the small firms sector for the UK economy. [8 marks]
   (b) Explain how supply-side policies have helped to improve the performance of the UK small firms sector. [12 marks]
2. (a) Discuss the factors which promote entrepreneurship. [8 marks]
   (b) Assess the impact of deregulation, privatisation and state education on the promotion of entrepreneurship. [12 marks]

Data response question

This task is based on a question set by Edexcel in 1997.

The following table and passage are extracts from a 1995 Monopolies and Mergers Commission Report into the supply of bus services in North East England.

Market Shares of Bus Companies in North East England

Bus company	Turnover (% share)	Vehicle miles (% share)
Stagecoach:		
Busways	25.6	19.9
Cleveland Transit	5.4	4.0
Hartlepool Transport	1.9	1.6
Total Stagecoach	32.9	25.5
Go-Ahead	28.4	28.1
North East Bus	16.7	18.9
British Bus	11.0	10.9
Others	11.0	16.6

Our investigations raised questions about the extent and nature of competition in the bus industry. In the North East we found little evidence of active competition between large operators; indeed the evidence of several parties (Busways, Go-Ahead, Yorkshire Traction, DCC) suggested that large operators consciously refrained from competing against each other. They appear to take the view that, in what is still a declining market in most areas, if hostilities were to break out between two large operators both would be worse off as a result, at least in the short term. Active competition takes place between small operators, or between a large and a small operator.

The nature of competition involving small operators may or may not, however, be helpful to the travelling public. We found examples where entrants had opened up routes which were at least partly new and had charged lower fares than the incumbent. These were, however, the exceptions; in most cases entry led to more services being run on routes which were already reasonably well served, usually close to the time of the existing service and at the same fares. Such competition can lead to congestion, pollution and instability of services as the competitors jockey for position, and provides little or no benefit to the travelling public.

These remarks are not intended to cast doubt on the importance of potential competition. Even if active competition between large groups is rare, their co-existence in adjacent and, in some places (eg Darlington), overlapping territories is likely to have some effect in discouraging abuse of locally dominant positions.

There are two factors which appear to create difficulties for the operation of the competitive process in the bus industry. First, it is difficult for suppliers to differentiate their products in a way which significantly influences customer choice. Put simply, passengers will generally board the first bus for their destination which comes and will not be prepared to wait for a later bus which may be more comfortable or may even charge lower fares (unless the difference is large). It is therefore possible for small, under-capitalised operators with old buses to abstract revenue on a significant scale from incumbents offering a more comprehensive and reliable service using modern vehicles. As a result, large operators tend to take the view that the only fully effective response to competitive entry in their territory is to eliminate the entrant.

This leads to the second point, which is that it is easy for a large operator to target a small one. The routes from which a small operator derives its revenue are obvious and can readily be attacked by selective fare-cutting and service introductions. Although entry is easy, it may be deterred if strong incumbents gain a reputation for 'seeing off' competitive incursions.

Meanwhile the rapid process of consolidation experienced since deregulation is continuing. The consensus among our witnesses was that the industry would come to be dominated by a small number – perhaps four to six – of large groups operating across many areas, with very few medium-sized operators but many small ones operating in particular localities.

As is widely recognised, deregulation of the bus industry has brought both benefits and disadvantages. The table below quantifies some of these.

Bus industry trends since deregulation

	Change since 1985/86(%)
Real operating costs per vehicle mile	−42
Vehicle miles run	+24
Real operating costs per passenger journey	0
Real fares	+17
Real passenger receipts	−10
Passenger numbers	−27
Real earnings of bus and coach drivers	−12
Real total government spending on local bus services (incl. London)	−31
Real spending by local authorities on local bus services	−55

Source: *The supply of bus services in the North East of England*, Cmd.2933, HMSO, August 1995

(a) With reference to the passage, what is the nature of price and non-price competition in the market for bus transport?

[10 marks]

(b) Examine the advantages and disadvantages of deregulation.

[20 marks]

(c) To what extent is the market for bus transport 'contestable'?

[20 marks]

Chapter Eight

External influence of supply-side policies and performance

'Overall the Single Market has yet to result in the transformation of the supply-side of the EU economy that its supporters promised.'
Iain Begg, 1998

Introduction
Although Britain has attempted to address its supply-side problems with varying levels of success, its supply-side performance has been subject to an increasing number of external forces, not least its membership of the European Union. Through the process of competition policy, the Single European Market, regional policy and other policy initiatives, the EU has sought to strengthen its own supply-side. These policy approaches have not always been welcomed by Britain which has often sought to develop a much more hands-off approach to the working of the market mechanism. Outside of the European framework, changes brought in by GATT and the WTO have also had profound effects on UK industry, as has also the encouragement of Foreign Direct Investment into Britain as a means to overcome its own problems with de-industrialisation and its structural weaknesses.

The Single European Market
In the period 1958–72 the European Community (EC; the EC became the European Union after the Maastricht Treaty in 1992) saw very fast growth rates as tariffs were reduced between member countries. Gradually, EC growth rates began to slow, partly as a result of tariff barriers being replaced by non-tariff barriers to trade. It appeared that we had a Community which was made up of countries operating independently. The fundamental problem for the EU was that centuries of separate political development by the twelve member states had spawned a dozen mutually inconsistent sets of legislation regarding technical and health and safety standards, segmenting the EU into small, discrete markets served by small-scale producers.

Moreover, European industry was beginning to lose market share to the US, Japan, and the emerging Tiger Economies of South East Asia, as their tariff protection sustained small, inefficient national producers

Table 13 The 1992 package of measures

Non-tariff barriers at which proposals are aimed	Number of proposals
Technical barriers and harmonisation	78
Veterinary and phytosanitary	83
Financial services and capital market controls	26
Free movement of persons	21
Control of goods	10
Transport	11
Indirect taxation	22
Public procurement	6
Telecom	5
Intellectual property	8
Company law	12
Total	**282**

from outside competition. Furthermore, unemployment was at a higher level than in the US and Japan, and the EC's inflation performance was also disappointing. Against this background the EC began to press for more unification and at the Copenhagen Summit in 1982 the heads of state agreed to make this a priority. In 1985 the White Paper, 'Completing the Internal Market', was issued, giving details of the proposal for the single market. Subsequently, the 1986 **Single European Act** (SEA) was adopted by the then 12 members, so committing themselves to market unification by the end of 1992. The Act agreed on a programme containing 300 separate pieces of legislation (subsequently reduced to 282) which would bring about a single market by the end of 1992. Table 13 sets out the package of legislative changes that the EU proposed to implement.

These directives were basically statements of the required outcome, and how this outcome could be achieved, but the legislation necessary for this was left to the individual members. No attempt was made to develop EC-wide targets, which had hampered such attempts in the past, and the idea of 'sufficient harmonisation' was put forward and extended to the concept of '**mutual recognition**' and 'approximation', thereby giving national governments some room for manoeuvre.

Main barriers pre-SEM
The areas which the SEM sought to address can be grouped under a number of broad headings:

Table 14 Excise duty per pint of beer in the UK and neighbouring brewing countries

Country	Excise duty
France	4.2p
Germany	4.4p
Luxembourg	4.5p
Belgium	7.9p
Netherlands	9.6p
UK	30.7p

Source: Brewers and Licensers Retail Association, 1996.

- **Physical barriers** – these included customs controls and formalities that imposed form filling costs, red tape administration costs and border delays.
- **Fiscal barriers** – the lack of harmonisation of VAT rates and excise duties (see Table 14).
- **Technical barriers** – obstacles to the free movement of goods, services, labour, capital and the issue of public procurement.

Most analysts believed the advantages to European business from the SEM were derived from:

- wider availability of economies of scale in the production process;
- the effects of more intense competition;
- lower barriers to entry;
- gains from reduction in X inefficiency;
- trade creation.

The costs centred on:

- adverse regional multiplier effects;
- the problems of radical economic change that can occur through efficiency and scale gains;
- alterations in the mode and manner in which firms alter their logistical chain.

Assessing the outcome of the SEM
One of the main features of the SEM was the **merger and takeover cycle** that followed. This was generated by the increase in cross-border mergers and through the move by companies outside of the EU needing to be inside what they felt might become 'Fortress Europe'. Such moves might be seen as reducing the possible benefits that might arise through increased competition.

Inevitably, the impact of the SEM is bound up in the extent to which the legislation has actually been implemented (see Table 15).

In terms of trade, the SEM programme has led to increasing intra-EU imports for both manufacturing and services, with the rise in the former being half as much as the rise in the latter. There have also been increases in **trade creation** relative to **trade diversion**, though the effects depend upon which sector is more sensitive to trade. Intra-industry trade has been strengthened relative to inter-industry trade, suggesting a move away from member state specialisation towards more symmetric industrial structures. This reduces the impact of asymmetric shocks – an important feature of the **Single currency**. Finally, there does not appear to be a case for core areas within the EU attracting more investment away from the peripheral areas.

Efficiency and competition effects of the SEM

There has been much advancement in the areas of efficiency and competition due to the substantial restructuring of European industries, though this has not been as large as forecast. Few of the efficiency gains can be related to technical improvements; many result from economies of scale through fixed investments in marketing, brand development, R&D expenditure and the development of new produc-

Table 15 Non-implementation of the SEM rules, 2 February 1999 (%)

Country	Non-implementation – all directives
Belgium	5.0
Denmark	1.1
Germany	2.5
Spain	1.8
Greece	4.8
France	4.4
Eire	4.6
Italy	5.1
Luxembourg	4.9
Netherlands	1.9
Austria	1.9
Portugal	5.5
Finland	0.7
Sweden	1.3
UK	2.7

Source: European Commission.

tive processes. Competition has intensified in many sectors with price reductions being passed on to consumers, but there are still large price differentials across the EU particularly with consumer goods and the equipment goods industries. Generally, the more goods and services are traded, the greater the price convergence. Price convergence is expected to increase as the full effects of both the SEM and European Monetary Union feed through.

Employment, income and convergence and the SEM

The EU Commission (1996) has calculated that the SEM has added 1.1 per cent to the growth rate of the EU and created around 300,000 jobs during the period 1985–95. However, it should be noted that isolating the effect of the SEM from other changes that have taken place in the EU is problematic. Investment is estimated to have increased by 1 per cent more than it would have done without the SEM and inflation is between 1 and 1.5 per cent less.

Impact on manufacturing

The effects of the SEM have not been uniform across the manufacturing sectors. The greatest effects have been in textiles, chemicals and motor vehicles where the SEM has accounted for 80 per cent of the changes in market share of intra-EU imports. The impact of the SEM on FDI will be considered later in this chapter, but in anticipation of the SEM, EU manufacturing exhibited a high level of merger and acquisition behaviour. Two-thirds of this was made up from domestic mergers and takeovers.

Between 1985 and 1992, there has been an increase in firm size within manufacturing in all large EU states except the UK. This growth in firm size appears to be in sectors unaffected by the SEM, suggesting that it is the intensity of competition rather than the SEM that was the main driving factor behind firm size. There is no evidence that enterprises have re-organised production and increased the size and scale of their growing operations as a result of the SEM.

Because the SEM has increased the intensity of competition within manufacturing it has imposed significant constraints upon price-cost margins of the magnitude of 1 per cent per annum since 1986. Not surprisingly, the reductions in price are to be found in those sectors that are more sensitive to the changes brought by the SEM, though the effects have extended beyond these sectors through networking and strategic reactions.

Impact on services

The SEM was successful in establishing a legal framework for services. However, because many of the measures have only come into place since 1993 it is probably too soon to assess both their full and partial effects. The problem is not helped by the uneven implementation of the legislation, however. It is important to note that since the introduction of the SEM, intra-EU trade in services has increased on average by 3.1 per cent per annum. Although there are difficulties in measuring the efficiency gains within this sector, those gains that are likely to have taken place are in the service sectors most exposed to the changes brought about by the SEM, for example distribution. Although the SEM has influenced technological changes in banking, other sectors have not greatly been affected, for example airlines. On the whole the efficiency gains from the SEM have been more as a result of changes in the domestic economies of the individual states, such as national privatisations and deregulation. Once again the overall direct impact of the SEM has been more disappointing than first envisaged.

There is no doubt that the SEM has had effects internally on organisations within the EU in varying degrees. But the SEM was also developed to improve competition and efficiency, and the development of markets through the encouragement of non-EU companies to enter the EU, and for those non-EU organisations which were already inside the EU at the inception of the EU to expand their activities. Thus the SEM had important effects on FDI within the EU and within the UK. So how has FDI altered in Europe and what has been the role of the SEM on this?

Foreign Direct Investment

Foreign Direct Investment (FDI) is investment in the business or financial affairs of another country that involves a strong element of (potential or actual) direct control of these activities. This foreign direct investment can come through mergers and takeovers, through the development of greenfield sites and through the expansion of existing sites. It is also important to distinguish between the net flow and stock of FDI and also to consider both its theoretical and actual impact on the UK economy.

Level of FDI activity in the UK

With just 1 per cent of the world's population, Britain obtains nearly 8 per cent of the world's cross-border direct investment. Only the US, with four times the UK's population, does better. In 1998, Britain's stock of FDI was $274bn (nearly double that in Germany), and out of the EU total of FDI stock the UK accounted for almost 23 per cent. This share had fallen back from 30 per cent a decade earlier. Of the stock of FDI in the UK, 44 per cent is from the US, with the top six European countries such as Germany, France and the Netherlands accounting for a further 35 per cent. Japan and Australia hold around 4 per cent each. Nearly 50 per cent of UK exports and 25 per cent of British output are now sourced from foreign companies.

If we turn to the flow of FDI, the UK remained the top destination for FDI in Europe, attracting almost 26 per cent of the overall flow into the EU between 1987 and 1998. In 1998–99, 652 new investments were made in Britain, valued at £40bn, creating or safeguarding 118,000 jobs. Increasingly, the UK is being targeted by FDI from Germany and France. Table 16 shows some of the important features of FDI in the UK. In particular it shows that mergers/acquisitions have played a growing part in FDI activity, responding to the SEM amongst

Table 16 Foreign Direct Investment (FDI) into the UK

Year	Stock of FDI*	Flow of FDI	Mergers/ acquisitions as a % of FDI	% of employees in manufacturing employed by foreign-owned enterprises	FDI as a proportion of total investment
1984	38 484	–245	–	14.8	–
1985	–	4 417	–	14.0	–
1986	–	5 645	21	13.0	–
1987	58 430	8 986	26	13.4	–
1988	71 652	11 562	23	13.1	–
1989	93 554	17 405	62	14.9	16.7
1990	105 760	17 155	58	16.1	16.2
1991	111 373	8 418	51	17.2	8.7
1992	114 409	8 816	38	18.1	9.2
1993	121 005	9 871	42	17.9	10.2
1994	121 336	6 046	74	18.6	5.7
1995	128 885	12 654	88	17.2	11.1
1996	134 654	15 662	41	–	13.2
1997	156 969	21 751	53	–	16.9
1998	–	–	–	–	26.2

Sources: Office of National Statistics, DTI, *International Direct Investment Year Book.*
*Data on stocks of FDI were collected only triennially before 1987.

other factors. In employment terms, FDI has become of growing importance as employers in the UK labour market.

Why does FDI come to Britain? First, Britain is a member of the EU, and most companies that locate in Britain from North America or Asia do so because of easy access to EU markets. But this does not explain why companies come to Britain as opposed to Germany or France. Additional specific British factors would include: the UK's reputation for innovation and its technological and financial expertise; its business-friendly tax system, culture and regulatory system; the liberalised telecommunications market; the availability of relatively cheap skilled labour; the high density of its population thus increasing consumer demand; the excellent labour relations since the early 1980s; and the English language.

The evidence from other countries suggests that labour flexibility is not the overriding factor behind FDI location. France has received large amounts of inward investment since the 1990s while the UK has been the single most important investor in France.

Longer term prospects for UK FDI

Will the popularity of Britain as a destination for FDI continue? Some have argued that Britain is the first destination for FDI by companies setting up in Europe and if this proves successful, further FDI expansion takes place elsewhere within the EU. The UK's decision not to enter the European single currency could act as a disincentive for some potential foreign investors. This was one of the reasons why Toyota invested FF4bn in a greenfield plant at Valenciennes in northern France in December 1997 rather than expand its investment in the UK, though the prospect of generous state subsidies may also have played their part. The figures for FDI inflows into sectors such as financial services, chemicals, the car industry and the like may show no downturn as yet, but the fear is that many of these investors are gambling on the UK joining the single currency in the short-to-medium term. Hesitation in the longer term may have damaging effects on FDI inflows. There is also evidence during the 1990s that Belgium, Netherlands and Ireland have received more inward investment per capita than the UK, and that once a country embraces full European integration, such as Spain and Sweden, they become more attractive for inward investment. In addition, the introduction of a minimum wage and the development of UK labour market regulations more along the lines that exist in continental Europe may also prove problematic. However, the UK is likely to still have the least regulated labour market compared with its major European competitors.

The type of inward investment into Britain is also changing. There is a move from big greenfield projects by global manufacturers to smaller investments by existing current foreign organisations. In addition there is also a change from greenfield site FDI to FDI through the merger and takeover of UK companies. In 1998, a third of FDI and almost half the jobs from FDI came from the takeover of UK companies. In this way foreign organisations are able to acquire and remove excess capacity in the European market. Moreover, there is a shift in FDI towards knowledge-based projects, such as information technology services for the internet, telecommunications, biosciences and pharmaceuticals, key areas outlined in the government's Trade and Industry Department's Competitiveness White Paper (1998). Some would argue that this sea change is way overdue since Britain has fared well in attracting relatively labour-intensive investments, but has been relatively backward in attracting more capital-intensive or R&D-intensive investments. Countries such as Germany, France and Ireland with well-educated and more numerate workforces and higher levels of technical skills often attract such investments.

Impact of FDI on UK economy

FDI appears to be a catalyst for output growth, capital accumulation and technological progress in the long term. FDI has much to offer the UK in terms of direct and indirect employment, the transfer of technology and improvements in managerial and operational skills. The contribution of foreign manufacturing to regional job creation has been well established, the crucial question is the role of FDI in terms of potential **dynamic gains** and as sources of growth for the economy. FDI might improve the technological base of a locality and thereby attract further high-quality inward investment. The spill-over effects might encourage further development in local firms improving both their domestic and international competitiveness. Alternatively, the more productive foreign organisations might use their advantages to damage domestic company sales and profitability. The superiority of foreign-owned companies in relation to their productivity is evidenced in the UK census of production. But there is also evidence that this superiority has been positively associated with the labour productivity of that industry. If foreign-owned firms, located in Britain and employing British workers, use high human and physical intensity to achieve high productivity, why don't British-owned establishments do the same? There are a number of possible answers.

- British firms may face a higher cost of capital, both externally and internally. This may not be a constraint for large companies but it may have credence for small and medium-sized enterprises.

- British firms may face less favourable risk-return trade-off than foreign ones and consequently may prefer less capital-intensive technologies.
- Foreign companies may use superior technology and business methods which happen to be more intensive in both capital and skilled labour.

But wouldn't British industry learn from the approaches adopted by foreign organisations? The answer may be yes, but suppose they are slow to learn, then the competitive advantages stay with foreign organisations for a long time. It is also possible to argue that foreign firms possessing competitive advantages, and often in the possession of a further subsidy in terms of government grants, are merely acting to replace a domestic monopoly with a foreign-owned one.

FDI impact on exports and employment

FDI also affects export potential. From being a net importer of both cars and televisions, Britain, through the impact of FDI, has become a net exporter of both products. At the same time, it is noticeable that Britain does not possess any domestically owned mainstream producers of the two products. However, Britain is also an important destination for outward FDI flows and this may have damaged Britain's export position.

Inward investment can also have impacts on employment. In the period 1986–92 there was a loss of 45,000 domestic jobs due to inward investment, balanced against the creation of 165,000 jobs in foreign organisations. The impact of FDI can also be seen in terms of closing the productivity gap. About three-quarters of the productivity gap between the UK, France and Germany was closed during the 1980s, and an appreciable amount of this was due to FDI, particularly FDI from the US.

There is little evidence that foreign investments in non-manufacturing sectors have generated beneficial supply-side improvements, apart from in the petroleum industry. It is not clear how foreign ownership of water companies and railway operators confers significant benefits on host economies. In addition, the switch towards mergers/takeovers as a source of FDI makes UK organisations more susceptible to closure (see Motorola), since it is much easier to shut down a plant in another country. If FDI is not embedded in the local economy the spill-over effects are much weaker and this too makes investment fragile.

Finally, it should be noted that FDI can also be outward from the UK economy as well as inward; in 1999, British firms invested £212bn overseas, more even than the US. Empirical evidence suggest that outward investment worsens UK export performance.

It is true that Britain attracts a proportionately large amount of mobile investment. With just 1 per cent of the world's population, it consumes nearly 8 per cent of all direct cross-border investment, second only to the US. In Europe, the UK is the self-proclaimed inward investment champion, gobbling up half the available total, compared with a meagre 5 per cent for France and 3 per cent for Germany.

The figures are huge. In 1998 foreign companies invested £40 billion in the UK, according to the United Nations Conference on Trade and Development. As many as 25,000 UK companies are estimated to be under foreign ownership, and 25 per cent of 'British' output comes from foreign-owned factories.

So that's all right, then. Well, not quite. Inward investment has gone unchallenged for so long as a plank of economic policy that people have forgotten to ask the more troubling questions. If foreign direct investment (FDI) is such a good thing, why is it only the UK that makes such a big thing of it? What does all the investment consist of? And what does it say about the functioning of the British economy as a whole?

The truth is that like so much of British management under scrutiny this 'triumph' is not nearly as wonderful as it seems. In the first place, much FDI activity represents mergers and acquisitions, which have replaced greenfield investment building new factories as the largest component of inward investment in developed countries.

The implications of foreign ownership and the unsympathetic economic policy are horribly illustrated by the Rover debacle. In that situation, where would you like the decisions made, Munich or Birmingham?

By the same token, the vaunted 'clusters' of foreign investment in the North East or 'Silicon Glen' are fragile things.

None of this is to deny the economic benefits that some inward investment provides. The National Institute of Economic and Social Research (NIESR) estimates that a third of UK industrial productivity growth since the mid-1980s can be attributed to the 'ripple-through' effect of better work practices imported by the incomers, principally the Japanese. Despite the strength of sterling, Japanese implants have also done much to sustain export figures in sectors such as cars and electronics.

But there is no such thing as a free lunch. Why has Johnny Foreigner (with the exception of BMW) been able to make a go of industries which British companies are abandoning in droves, such as cars, electronics, televisions, utilities? Why has it taken foreign management to restore a measure of credibility to British quality and British labour?

A large part of the answer lies in vastly better management at every level. For foreign firms, the opportunity to buy cheap assets and cheap labour with which to compete in a wildly over-priced UK market is a no-brainer, particularly since ease of entry and investment are matched by ease of exit.

Meanwhile, spurning the opportunities on their doorstep, UK firms have become the world leaders in exporting capital. Last year they invested a towering $212bn overseas, more even than the US.

Simon Caulkin, adapted from, 'Inwardly troubled',
The Observer, 16 April 2000

Deregulation in Europe

In Chapter 4 we discussed the role that privatisation has played in the UK, but after a slow start this has also caught on in the rest of Europe. Both in eastern and western Europe, banking, telecommunications and energy sectors have been transferred from public to private ownership. Between 1993 and 1998, Italy (£56bn), France (£36bn), Spain (£28bn) and Germany (£23bn) were all ahead of the UK (£22bn) in terms of the receipts from privatisations. But more profound changes have also taken place within the EU which have impacted upon Britain's supply-side performance. There have been moves to deregulate or liberalise a range of markets.

Within the EU, the telecommunications market has been liberalised since 1998, the result of which has been a wider range of services and lower call costs. This also triggered off a wave of merger activity in this sector, one of the biggest being between Germany's Deutsche Telecom AG and Telecom Italia. It has been shown that telecoms traffic grows twice as fast in competitive markets as monopoly markets and the benefits flow to all corners of the economy in the form of new technology, innovative services, lower distribution costs and much lower average tariffs. In early 1999, Europe also gave electricity customers the right to choose a supplier other than their local monopoly. This may only apply to large industrial users at the moment but the intention is that it will be extended to every consumer in every country. This deregulation is intended to boost competition in electricity markets. In the airline industry, the result of deregulation and liberalisation has led to the development of a number of low cost operators such as Easy Jet, Go, and Ryan Air. Once again, as the market has opened up national carriers have turned to mergers, takeovers and strategic alliances to protect their markets. Even in the rail industry the partial deregulation of the rail freight industry has taken place.

Much of the deregulation and liberalisation of markets in Europe has only been a recent phenomenon – some would see it as one of the final pieces of the SEM. In the short term, we may notice very little change in some of the sectors deregulated or liberalised, particularly as a number of governments are dragging their feet as a way of protecting their state-owned enterprises. It remains to be seen whether these supply-side changes need a further push from government or will develop a momentum of their own.

Supply-side changes and international trade agreements

The changes that arose through the 'single market' encouraged trade between the EU member states. However, on a wider international stage, 'supply-siders' have seen the great benefits that could be achieved by continuing to remove barriers to trade in a global sense.

The eighth GATT round – the **Uruguay Round** – attempted to develop and widen the issues and areas that would help to liberalise markets. The results of the trade talks have been estimated to have brought an increase in world GDP by about 1 per cent. The 'successful' conclusion of the Uruguay Round also led to the setting up of the **World Trade Organisation (WTO)** as the successor to GATT in 1995. The WTO has appeared to be fairly successful. Membership of the organisation has grown by almost 50 countries, thereby improving global trade. It has a stronger disputes settlement mechanism and has more ability to enforce its rulings, with the new rules applying to all signatories not just the industrialised countries. However, there are still problems. It has been argued, particularly by the EU, that the US has introduced its own trade reprisals without going through WTO procedures. Furthermore, substantial barriers to trade still exist and countries fear the effect of opening up markets because of the effect it will have on their domestic industries. One area in particular is still subject to large amounts of protection – agriculture.

The new round of trade talks

It is against this background, and with the development of more and more regional trading blocks that a new round of trade talks has been developed – the **Seattle Trade Talks**. The big problem for the Seattle Round as it has been called, is the agenda. Under the 1994 Uruguay Round agreement there was a built-in agenda which specified future trade areas that needed revision. For example, by 2000 it was agreed that both agriculture and services would be looked at again since a number of the proposals agreed to under the Uruguay Round would be close to running out at that point. Many countries want the new talks to focus on these areas alone. The developed nations, however, want the trade talks to be much wider, including technical barriers to trade, electronic commerce, trade and labour, trade in services investment, government procurement and the like. Furthermore, there is perhaps a need to address some of the deficiencies with the outcome of the Uruguay Round itself, such as making sure the disputes settlement mechanism works correctly, and reducing contingent protection. The Seattle conference, even with all its disruptions, did manage to close a number of gaps between the 135 member countries of the WTO, but there is still a great deal of distance between the parties.

Conclusion

Improving the supply-side of the economy has been an important policy area over the last thirty years, but equally as important as domestic government activity to improve the supply-side has been the effects on British economic performance through external factors and membership of trading and economic bodies. The SEM attempted to deal with Europe's relatively poor supply-side performance. There is no doubt that this has worked but not to the degree envisaged. The move to a fully integrated internal market in the light of the move towards monetary union has received further commitment through the development of a new Action Plan to secure completion of the SEM.

Alongside the SEM came the deregulation of a number of sectors within the EU. At present the results from these can be said to be a little disappointing, not least due to the member states dragging their feet over the liberation of air traffic, energy and telecommunications. Thus deregulation in these sectors is only a recent phenomenon and the full impact on competition is yet to be seen. At the same time as the SEM was coming into operation, the industrialised countries signed up to the Uruguay trade Round. Once again results have been a little disappointing. Trade and competition has increased but not to the extent envisaged. The Seattle Trade Talks have attempted to address some of the unfinished business of the Uruguay Round, yet the speed with which the global economy is changing probably requires more fundamental changes. It is failure to agree on the extent of these fundamental changes that is holding up progress.

Finally, this chapter has examined the role of FDI in improving Britain's supply-side performance. FDI can bring many positive changes to the host economy, yet there is doubt being raised about the footloose nature of Britain's FDI and whether it is bringing the types of jobs and goods at the leading edge of the market.

KEY WORDS

Single European Act	Single currency
Mutual recognition	Foreign Direct Investment
Physical barriers	Dynamic gains
Fiscal barriers	The Uruguay Round
Technical barriers	World Trade Organisation
Merger and takeover cyccle	(WTO)
Trade creation	The Seattle Trade Talks
Trade diversion	

Further reading

Bamford, C. and Grant, S. (2000), Chapters 5 and 8 in, *The UK Economy in a Global Context*, Studies in Economics and Business, Heinemann Educational.

Chapman, I. (2000), 'What is the importance of inward investment to the UK economy?', *Economics Today*, Vol. 7, No. 3, January.

Hill, B. (2001), Chapters 6 and 7 in, *The European Union*, 4th edn, Studies in Economics and Business, Heinemann Educational.

Ingham, B. and Abu Shair, (1998), 'The World Trade Organisation: trade and protection in a changing world economy', in *Developments in Economics Annual Review*, ed. A.G. Atkinson, Vol. 14.

Smith, D. (1999), Chapter 9 in *UK Current Economy Policy*, 2nd edn, Studies in Economics and Business, Heinemann Educational.

Useful websites

WTO: www.wto.org

FDI-Southcentre: www.Southcentre.org/publications/fdi/fdi%20final%20trans–03.htm

Conclusion

'Supply-side economics [is] common sense ... Economists have long recognised the importance of an economy's productive capacity – its stock of labour and capital and the incentives needed to get the best out of them ... Marx was in many respects a supply-side economist.'
The Economist

There is nothing new about 'supply-side economics'. Although the term, 'supply-side economics' came into common usage only relatively recently, the idea that governments should direct economic policies towards strengthening the supply-side dates back to Adam Smith. Indeed, according to Colin Harbury and Richard Lipsey,

> *'supply-side economics ... is what Adam's Smith's "Wealth of Nations" was all about'.*

The argument has always been over the best means to achieve the end of a vital supply-side, rather than over the end itself.

Until the 1930s, governments believed that the best way to promote economic growth was to provide a stable, *laissez-faire* business environment in which private sector activity could flourish. During the depression of the interwar years, faith in the ability of free markets to deliver economic prosperity was badly dented. The so-called 'Keynesian revolution' overturned the apparently discredited classical orthodoxy, encouraging postwar governments to intervene directly in the supply-side to achieve their objectives for growth.

In recent years, however, the pendulum has come full circle, with the new classical 'counter-revolution' challenging the Keynesian approach to the supply-side. Under the guidance of new classical economists, governments around the world have set about dismantling the apparatus of state regulation and control, in an attempt to breathe life back into the market forces they charge excessive governments with having suffocated.

In the UK, the results of this intellectual backlash against state intervention in the supply-side have been mixed. Output and productivity growth both improved in the 1980s relative to the period 1973–79, but failed to regain the momentum enjoyed during the 1960s – when Keynesianism was at its zenith. In fact, during the late 1990s, the UK still appeared to be unable to bridge the productivity gap with its major competitors. Industrial relations have undoubtedly benefited from the new legislative framework introduced during the 1980s and

121

1990s and strikes have fallen to record lows. This has still been the case as the UK enters the new millennium. On the other hand, investment in both physical and human capital (training and education) remains well below the levels taken for granted in other advanced economies and R&D is on a downward trend.

Against this background, the indications are that a process of convergence towards a more balanced approach to supply-side policy is likely to prevail for the near future. While new classical, free market policies have strengthened the supply-side in certain areas (eg, labour relations), the experience of the 1980s and 1990s has revealed important limitations in the *laissez-faire* philosophy. Some types of economic activity are plagued by market failure: private companies are loath to train workers, since it is more cost-effective (at the level of the individual company) to free-ride in the hope that rivals will train staff that can subsequently be poached; similarly, it is cheaper to wait for other firms to pay for pioneering R&D, producing cheaper imitation products once the new technology has been perfected.

There is no doubt that supply-side changes have caused major changes in the UK economy, and this can be seen in the context of reduced unemployment coupled with a stable level of inflation, increased participation in higher education and less internal, through growing external, skill shortages. The UK has also benefited with regard to its supply-side from the continued flow of FDI. However, supply-side changes are unlikely to give immediate results within the context of the economy, their effect is more likely to be seen in the medium-to-long term. Perhaps more important is that supply-side policies have still left significant problems for the UK to overcome. These include low levels of numeracy and basic skills and the need to develop better the innovative and entrepreneurial culture of the UK. Just when supply-side policies appeared to be addressing one range of weaknesses in the UK economy so another set of problems showed up. This suggests that the improvements in the UK economy achieved so far are just the start of a long process and there is still much to do to shake the UK out of its malaise.

Index